Edited by Sally Smith January–April 2018

The Bible Reading Fellowship
15 The Chambers, Vineyard
Abingdon OX14 3FE
brf.org.uk

The Bible Reading Fellowship (BRF) is a Registered Charity (233280)

ISBN 978 0 85746 608 2

Acknowledgements
Scripture quotations taken from The Holy Bible, New International Version (Anglicised edition) copyright © 1979, 1984, 2011 by Biblica. Used by permission of Hodder & Stoughton Publishers, a Hachette UK company. All rights reserved. 'NIV' is a registered trademark of Biblica. UK trademark number 1448790.

Scripture quotations from The New Revised Standard Version of the Bible, Anglicised edition, copyright © 1989, 1995 by the Division of Christian Education of the National Council of the Churches of Christ in the United States of America. Used by permission. All rights reserved.

Extract from *As a Child* by Phil Steer, published by lulu.com, 2012.

Every effort has been made to trace and contact copyright owners for material used in this resource. We apologise for any inadvertent omissions or errors, and would ask those concerned to contact us so that full acknowledgement can be made in the future.

Printed by Gutenberg Press, Tarxien, Malta

Sally Smith writes...

Welcome to this issue of *Quiet Spaces*!

This issue will take you through Lent and Easter and into celebrating the resurrection of Christ. Lent is often taken as a time for learning and for exercising discipline, so we are offering a focus on different ways of praying and inviting you to spend time trying them and learning more about praying in these ways. You will find that some come more readily to you than others – that's because we are all different and have different preferences and strengths. It does not mean that any one way is superior to any other way.

Similarly, how we approach these sections will vary. Some of you may want to keep with one section and follow it through, learning through the repeated practice and experience. Others of you may prefer to mix and match as you travel through Lent, taking forms of prayer that may challenge alongside those you know will feed and encourage. Again, either is fine, as long as you use *Quiet Spaces* to help you spend time with God and hear his voice. Some may be tempted to skip sections they anticipate as hard or 'not for me'. I would encourage you to try to avoid this. Growth often comes when there is challenge and it can be refreshing, though hard work, to explore new ways of praying.

Do enjoy lingering over those prayer forms that bring you to God, and refresh your skills in those you may have neglected and where you have become rusty. And remember, the ultimate aim is to encounter God and spend time in his presence, not to get to the end of the book!

So, prepare to be challenged, to experience the new and be comforted by the familiar. God knows you and will honour your commitment and openness, and he remains always the God of surprises.

Writers in this issue

Claire Musters is a freelance writer and editor, mother of two, pastor's wife and school governor. Claire's desire is to help others draw closer to God through her writing, which focuses on marriage, parenting, worship and issues facing women today. To find out more, visit www.clairemusters.com and @CMusters on Twitter.

Sue McCoulough worked for a number of years at the BBC. She was then Prayer Coordinator at the aid agency Tearfund, writing prayer materials and liaising with supporters. A reader at her church since 2000, she enjoys creative writing as well as organising and leading occasional retreats and Quiet Days.

Joy MacCormick, poet and New Zealand Anglican priest, has special concern for those who struggle to reconcile their experience of Holy Mystery with traditional church doctrine and teaching. Now retired from parish ministry, she continues to offer spiritual direction and supervision and to write. She is author of *Moments of Grace* (BRF, 2013).

Jean Sims offers spiritual accompaniment and enjoys leading Quiet Days, providing prayer spaces and guiding retreats. She belongs to the prayer and spirituality group in her diocese and helps to lead courses on prayer and in the training of spiritual directors for the Diocese of Southwell and Nottingham.

Liz Hoare is tutor in spiritual formation at Wycliffe Hall in Oxford. She teaches discipleship and prayer and has a special interest in spiritual direction. She is married to Toddy, a sculptor, and they have a son. Liz enjoys baking, the English countryside and looking after her chickens.

Lisa Cherrett is Production Editor at Bible Society, having worked as an editor at BRF for 19 years. She sings in a choir, writes haiku poetry when the inspiration strikes and enjoys making her own perfume. She blogs at lisannie44.wordpress.com.

Sally Smith enjoys creating spaces that enable encounters with God through leading Quiet Days and creating prayer corners and stations. She has led prayer groups in her local church, works as a spiritual director and writes and produces educational materials.

Janet Lunt is a musician by trade, arranging and typesetting music for publication. She runs St Peter's Hospice Community Choir in Bristol, and is involved in the musical aspect of worship, playing and composing. She also creates reflective prayer stations which are an integral part of her occasional Quiet Days.

Sally Welch is Vicar of Charlbury with Shorthampton and Area Dean of Chipping Norton in the Diocese of Oxford. She is a writer and lecturer on spirituality, and is particularly interested in pilgrimage and labyrinth. She has made many pilgrimages both in England and Europe.

Letting go of anxiety

Claire Musters

What the Bible says about worry

Introduction

> Worrying is carrying tomorrow's load with today's strength – carrying two days at once. It is moving into tomorrow ahead of time. Worrying does not empty tomorrow of its sorrow; it empties today of its strength.
>
> Corrie Ten Boom

I love that quote – it is so full of wisdom. But it also challenges me, because I know that so often I can allow worries about future events to overshadow my present.

While the Bible is full of instances of God telling us not to fear (he says it in various ways more than 350 times), most of us struggle at one time or another with fear or anxiety.

So what is it about worry that means it affects us even after we profess that we trust in God and will look to him for all our needs, as we seek to serve him faithfully?

It is reassuring that God knew that the human heart has a tendency to fall prey to worry. That's probably why he reminds us so often not to fear!

We can worry about so many things – how we are going to pay our rent/mortgage, what a meeting at work is going to be like, dealing with teenage children's hormones, getting enough sleep, etc… So why is such a 'natural', everyday thing as worry so deadly for us?

Worry affects us physically – there is research that shows it can weaken our immune system, cause heart disease, muscle tension, memory loss, respiratory disorders and digestive conditions.

But worry does so much more than that – it also affects us spiritually. When we allow fear to overtake us it also pushes away faith and, as a result, we start to feel cut off from God's presence. Sometimes the worry that causes the most problems is actually a general, unfounded, fear that overtakes our minds and blows things out of all proportion. We can feel that God can't possibly help – that's when we need to admit to ourselves that worry has taken over!

When fear takes hold

Bible story

Abraham is referred to as the Father of Nations. He is used as an example of deep faith in God – after all, when God told him to leave his homeland he responded with immediate obedience.

There are moments in his story, however, when we can see fear overtaking him. In those times, faith doesn't get a look in; for an example read Genesis 12:10–13.

At this point in their journey, Abram takes his family down to Egypt. He knows it is necessary because of the famine, but he doesn't trust God for his family's protection. Abram is scared that the Pharaoh will take a shine to his wife and will want her for himself. He responds out of that fear, asking Sarai to tell a half-truth – she was his half-sister (see Genesis 20:12), but, of course, she was also his wife.

As Sarai's brother, Abram would be treated with respect and shown kindness – as her husband his life would be in danger if Pharaoh did want to take Sarai to his harem, as he would stand in the way. So, concentrating on that fear, Abram's own self-preservation kicked in, and the practical steps he took showed he was no longer trusting in God.

Often the cause of our worry can be down to the fear of an outcome that we don't think we will like, and when we focus our hearts and minds on such a fear, our behaviour lines up to that rather than to God and his sovereignty.

Sadly, even though God dealt with the situation, caused Pharaoh to realise what he had done was wrong and enabled them to move on safely (see Genesis 12:14–20), Abraham repeated his mistake (in Genesis 20). Are there particular worries in your own life that cause you to take your eyes off God and which have you reacting out of fear? Ask God for forgiveness and spend some time worshipping him, declaring that he is sovereign and Lord over all.

What alleviates worry for you?

Creative

Proverbs 12:25 says 'Anxiety weighs down the heart, but a kind word cheers it up.'

It can be helpful to visualise the things that cause us worry or anxiety and the things we can do to alleviate them. Find a largeish piece of paper and some pens.

Draw a heart in the centre of the paper – this is going to be the central point of a pair of old-fashioned scales. Draw the line of the scales as a diagonal above the heart, so that the left-hand side is far down and the right-hand side much higher up. Write the word 'anxiety' at the lowest point (or draw a picture of what it is that makes you anxious), and then think about what things help you feel better when you are anxious and put those at the highest point (writing them as a list or drawing each one). These might include:

speaking to a friend, exercise, prayer, listening to worship music, but do include other things that you know are effective for you.

Once you have finished your scales picture, think about what one thing you would like to do from the right-hand list/pictures and take the time to do it today.

Turning worries to prayers

Prayer

I have heard many Christians over the years say that they can't help what they think about. But the truth is, God has taught us to 'be transformed by the renewing of your mind' (Romans 12:2). If our minds can be renewed, how does that happen? Scripture teaches us that we can 'take captive every thought to make it obedient to Christ' (2 Corinthians 10:5).

The first step is to learn to be more self-aware about what you are allowing your mind to dwell on. At regular intervals in the day, stop and reflect on what thoughts you have entertained in your mind – both the positive and negative.

If you discover your thoughts are mainly made up of worries, recall this quote from Corrie Ten Boom: 'Any concern too small to be turned into a prayer is too small to be made into a burden.'

We can take our worries, one by one, and turn them into prayers, so that we are asking God for his input and perspective on them. For example, if you are worried about whether you will meet a work deadline, you could pray:

Thank you, Lord, that you are in control of time. Help me to prioritise mine well. Keep me alert and my mind active and focused on the task in hand, so that I can meet this deadline. I don't want to do it in my own strength; rather, I want to include you in the process. Amen

Spend some time now praying instead of worrying!

Drinking in God's word – and his peace

Spotlight

There has been research in recent years looking specifically into how our brains work. It is fascinating to learn that our thoughts form connections in the brain, which the brain then filters by the strength of those thoughts. While we are asleep, anything that we have stopped thinking about, or haven't thought about much, is pruned as it is deemed not useful enough to keep. Scientists have concluded that what we think about and meditate on most during the day is reinforced while we sleep – while those things we do not think about much are 'deleted' from our brains. What a great advert for why meditation is so important!

A recent survey reported that the average family in the West owns three Bibles, and yet 80 per cent of Christians do not read their Bibles regularly. And we wonder why we struggle to locate specific verses when we want to find out what the Bible says about a particular situation we are facing! This really reinforces how meditating on scripture can be so helpful in combating worry. So let's do some...

Slowly read Philippians 4:6–8.

These particular verses highlight the importance of thinking about things that will uplift us, rather than drag us down. They also contain great advice – to take any anxieties straight to God. In the previous section we looked at how we can turn our worries into prayer and thanksgiving, and here we are also told what thoughts to focus on (or what to replace worry-filled thoughts with). Once we've given our worries to God in prayer, we need to give ourselves the space and time to drink in God's peace.

Make some space to receive God's peace yourself; you may like to sink into your favourite armchair, put on some relaxing music, light a candle – do whatever will relax you and then offer yourself to God afresh. Perhaps open your hands to show God you are ready to receive his peace. Spend as long as you need to with this.

If you would like to look at other scriptures that talk about the importance of meditating on God's word, try Joshua 1:8, Psalm 1:1–3, Psalm 119:1, Deuteronomy 11:18.

Using worry beads

Creative

Worry beads (*komboloi*) are widely available in Greece and Cyprus. The origins date back to when monks at Mount Athos began making strands of beads by tying knots on a string at regular intervals in order to say their prayers to God. However, in modern times the komboloi is usually used for fun and relaxation rather than for religious or ceremonial purposes.

The modern Greek word *komboloi* derives from *kombos* (knot) and *logio* (collection) or the verb *leo* (say). It is said that it is short for the phrase 'in every knot I say a prayer'. This etymology accounts for the fact that the *komboloi* actually evolved from *komboskini*, the Greek word for prayer rope.

One of the best ways that we can combat worry, as we have said, is by feeding our minds with truths. What better truths can we use than those focusing on God's character, and our standing before him?

Take some time to create your own set of 'worry beads', which you can then use whenever you feel you are beginning to get anxious. You could simply use string and purchase some fairly large beads, so that you can write on them (or you can buy different colours, and create a checklist on paper that you use alongside the beads, providing a different truth for each colour). If you choose to write on the beads you could simply write one word, which will then trigger the truth in your mind (such as 'loved'). Alternatively, you could cut out short strips of paper, write a truth on each one (such as 'God is love', 'I am God's beloved', 'God is my provider') and make a simple paper chain by looping and connecting them.

Seeing God's care in nature

Going out

Read Matthew 6:25–34.

> *Therefore I tell you, do not worry about your life, what you will eat or drink; or about your body, what you will wear.*
> Matthew 6:25

Make some time today to go for a walk, preferably in the countryside or a park. Take time to look at any birds you come across – their appearance, and also what they are doing. Consider how much detail God has put into creating them. Also, stop when you find some flowers, get down to eye level with them and take your time to look at all the details contained in them. Think of their petals, colour, etc. as 'clothes', as the Matthew passage describes, and reflect on how resplendently they are 'dressed'.

Now consider the fact that Jesus reminds us in our passage that we are so much more valuable to him than they are. Having pondered the great care God has taken in nature, how does that now make you feel? Spend some time with those feelings. You may like to then thank God for his abundant love.

Running scared and exhausted

Bible reading

Familiarise yourself with the story of Elijah by reading 1 Kings 18—19. In the first of these chapters we see how Elijah, God's prophet, defiantly challenges the prophets of Baal, in an attempt to get the people to stop wavering between worship of God and worship of Baal. With two altars prepared with sacrifices, Elijah invites the prophets of Baal to call on their god to burn up the offering. We see Elijah full of confidence here, even goading the prophets when they get no response (see 18:27). When it is time for him to pray to God, Elijah even pours water on his prepared altar, so sure is he that God will do a miracle. And he does. Afterwards, Elijah has the prophets of Baal killed.

When King Ahab tells Jezebel what Elijah has done, her response is to threaten Elijah's life (see 19:2). It seems incredible, after demonstrating such powerful faith, that he 'was afraid and ran for his life' (v. 3). And yet, even in our moments of heightened success, we can be vulnerable to anxiety and fear. Elijah was exhausted, depressed and gripped by fear – even though God had just given him a great victory.

We see how God looks after him: he sends an angel with food (vv. 5–8) and allows Elijah to rest. Even when refreshed, Elijah runs to hide in a cave. It is after he has rested that God confronts him and asks why he is there (v. 9). God then brings wind, an earthquake and a fire, and finally comes to Elijah through a gentle whisper, asking him the same question – why are you here? He speaks directly to Elijah's unfounded fears, pointing out that, while Elijah believes he is the only God-fearing prophet left, there are in fact 7,000. He then gives him instructions on what to do next, not disqualifying him because of his moment of fear.

I think there are many things we can learn from Elijah's life, not least that none of us are immune to fear and anxiety! It can often hit us directly after what we may view as a 'spiritual high point' in our lives; we need to be aware of that, and guard our hearts and minds.

God doesn't tell Elijah to snap out of his depression; rather, he provides for his basic physical needs and allows him to rest. When he does finally confront Elijah's wrong thinking, he does it through a quiet, gentle whisper. How often do we give ourselves the space to do as God asks us to in Psalm 46:10: 'Be still, and know that I am God'?

Whenever we are feeling pressurised or fearful we can approach God full of stress, desperate for a loud answer, and yet God often wants us to calm down, be still and get rested so that we can then listen out for his quiet wisdom.

Take a moment to think about how you purposefully position yourself to hear from God, particularly when you are anxious. Do you make space to be still, or do you frantically run around trying to deal with all the stresses of your day in your own strength, simply vocalising 'Help me!' prayers in the middle of all the mayhem?

Perhaps you need to take some time today to repent of anything that gets in the way of hearing God, and explore with him ways in which you can learn to 'be still'.

Taking our worries to the cross

Imaginative

We can take our worries to God by visualising ourselves before the cross. Make yourself comfortable and then:

Picture the cross – what does it look like? What surrounds it? How does God reveal his presence to you there? Spend some time just resting before the cross.

Now take one of your current worries to God by imagining laying it at the foot of the cross.

Watch God take that worry away so that you no longer need to pick it back up.

Remain by the cross, ready to receive any gift God may be offering to you. Perhaps the gift of peace, or a reassurance of his love for you.

Take time to soak in the atmosphere at the cross. How does it make you feel? How could you respond?

Order your day

Prayer

This is a very simple practice that I was encouraged to take on board a few years ago. The practice of ordering your day helps you to slow down in order to hear from God. It confronts that feeling of being overwhelmed and anxious about how much you have to fit into every day.

As someone who works from home, and only during the hours my children are at school, I have to be very disciplined and task-orientated. But that does mean I can get quite stressed about how much I need to get done each day. However, God recently challenged me to pray for him to order my day each morning.

I begin my working day by simply taking the time to worship God. I then call to mind all the items on my 'to do' list and take them to him in prayer, holding them lightly as I ask him to order my day. I ask him to let me know if I need to reprioritise or let anything go. I also ask him to keep me attentive towards anyone or anything that he wants me to add into my day.

Since doing this regularly I have found my days are completely different! I am less stressed and anxious about my workload as writing jobs have come together much more quickly than I'm expecting them to. I have also had more 'God-incidences' in my life – probably because my heart has been softened towards them so I notice and am able to acknowledge them. There have been moments when I've connected with someone in real need, and it has done us both such good and re-energised me.

But it has also allowed me not to be so precious about my task list too. Recently I was feeling under the weather and when I brought my day before God I felt him say my priority was 'self-care'. So I enjoyed a morning working from my bed, tackling a lot of the reading that I needed to do, and only later started working at my desk on the things I had set aside for the day.

If you have never tried praying 'Order my day', then I would urge you, in an attitude of humility, to try it. I have found it so freeing!

Remembering God's faithfulness

Creative

Finding ways of remembering God's faithfulness over the years helps lift our faith levels in those moments we feel shaky.

This practice is not new: God's people, the Israelites, passed down stories of God's faithfulness from generation to generation through stories and songs, which we can see throughout the Old Testament, such as in the Psalms – see 105 as an example – or in Nehemiah 9 where we see a time of corporate prayer in which God's people declare his faithfulness through recounting Israel's history.

If you have never used a journal before, can I encourage you today to purchase a nice notebook that you can use and set aside some time this week to write in it? You can use it to record whatever you want to: I often write out scriptures that speak to me from my daily readings, prayer requests and answers, words other people feel God is saying to me, etc.

If you use a journal regularly, try reflecting on God's faithfulness in your own life today by writing a song or poem in your journal, or look back through your journal and be encouraged by the times when God has been faithful to you.

Connecting with others

Story

Finally, we remind ourselves that God has put us into church families so that we can lean on one another in difficult times.

Often, when feeling anxious, we can default to wanting to hide away, but, in fact, gathering to pray with others can really help us when we are facing a stressful situation.

Last autumn my daughter had an extremely stressful half-term full of tests and auditions for secondary schools. Having supported her for over a year as she has studied for the entrance exams, I found on the day of the first one I could hardly concentrate – couldn't work – as it was so much on my mind. On the day of the second test, we were just finishing a week of prayer at church, so the whole family spent the morning with others from church enjoying an all-age prayer time, with worship, creative prayer stations, etc. My daughter left there to go to the exam having worshipped God and spent time praying with others – and as she arrived she bumped into another friend from church who was also sitting the exam so was able to go in with her (which was something I had specifically prayed about).

I dropped my daughter off and went straight back to church where I had a slot booked in the prayer room with some friends. We were able to pray for many different things both in our local area and internationally, but we stopped at the time her exam started, when she should have been having a break and when the second test paper would be starting, to cover both her and her friend in prayer. What a difference being surrounded by others who were also praying made! The whole day was so much more peaceful.

If you know you are going to be, or are, facing something that could make you anxious, take some time to think about who God has brought into your life that you trust, and ask them to pray with you.

The Lion, the Witch and the Wardrobe

Sue McCoulough

C.S. Lewis

Introduction

The Christian story has many instances of light coming out of darkness, so it's hardly surprising that C.S. Lewis's magical novel *The Lion, the Witch and the Wardrobe* was written in one of the gloomiest periods of his life. During the early 1950s Lewis had been passed over repeatedly for promotion at Oxford University. He'd struggled to cope with family illness and faced breakdown in his long-standing friendship with J.R.R. Tolkien.

So were the Narnia series of books written as a form of escapism? Alister McGrath in *Deep Magic, Dragons and Talking Mice* thinks not. He believes Lewis sought a creative project in 'Narnia' – something to combine fun storytelling with exploring theological ideas.

Lewis's struggle to come to faith is well documented. Like many early 20th-century Western intellectuals, he became an atheist after the horrors of World War I, believing that religious faith was untenable. However, a sense that rationalism was deeply unsatisfying to the human spirit grew within him. On finally coming to faith in the early 1930s, Lewis perceived that many, like him, had discounted Christianity without grasping its true message.

Lewis believed we live in a world shaped by stories. He increasingly explored the intellectual and imaginative appeal of Christianity – the links between faith and the imagination; between fact and myth. Hence he aimed to help readers see afresh what it means to be confronted by a living God. Like its successors in the Narnia series, *The Lion, the Witch and the Wardrobe* is a combination of Christian allegory and the kinds of children's story that Lewis read as a boy.

You might like to get the book off the shelf or find it in the library. If you know *The Lion, the Witch and the Wardrobe* well, do you have a favourite section? What does that tell you of God and your relationship with him?

Into the wardrobe

Reflective

Read 2 Corinthians 4 and 5.

The Pevensie children (Susan, Peter, Lucy and Edmund) enter two different worlds during *The Lion, the Witch and the Wardrobe*. Firstly, they leave their home as evacuees: a dislocating experience for many youngsters during World War II. Then they enter the completely different world of Narnia, inhabited by talking creatures. Dark forces are discovered there, as in their own war-torn country.

First Lucy, then Edmund and finally all four children together go beyond the wardrobe. As each experiences something different, so our personality, life situation and imaginative response lead us on differing faith journeys.

Open your own wardrobe door and gaze inside. Do you see what you expected to find? If clothes, what might they say about how you present yourself to the world? Are there matching colours and styles, or just a few items you 'mix and match' without much planning? Whether you're a careful dresser or not, do you confirm or challenge the world of 'appearances'?

Now dig a bit deeper into the wardrobe. Do you find unexpected items speaking of 'hidden' or forgotten things in your life? A large box sits at the back of my wardrobe containing old letters and cards from family and friends. I rarely re-read them, but am loath to bin them. So perhaps my 'hidden' life is sentimental, hankering after security, to hear 'voices from the past'.

Most believers long to go beyond the wardrobe of external appearances and seek true reality. Leaving the wardrobe, Lucy first arrives in a wood. I suspect this is a metaphor for a place where Christ's transformative power lies. However, dangers can lurk there, especially if we can't see the wood for the trees!

Spend time now touching the back of your wardrobe. Feel the wood, knock on it, perhaps. Sense how it's been transformed into furniture, solid and hidden, something rarely thought about. Let it point to a deeper space inside and beyond you – beyond self-consciousness, sentimental hankerings after the past, even future longings. Spend time asking Jesus where he'd like to bring transformation, as you mentally prepare to take a 'walk in the woods'.

Doorways into mystery

Imaginative

The Lion, the Witch and the Wardrobe speaks to adults and children alike who share experiences of entering another world. Wardrobes can be mundane pieces of furniture but yet are mysteriously 'deep'. Most of us as children played 'hide and seek' and wardrobes lend themselves to such games. As we grow older, we may use our imagination less and therefore find it difficult to comprehend God and his actions, in perpetual movement between this world and the next. Yet scripture says he came to live among us and continues to appear in a host of ways on earth. As Narnia reminds us, he also beckons us through a doorway into another ultimate world, heaven.

Visualise yourself becoming smaller, able to creep inside a wardrobe. Sense being invited to go beyond the rows of coats and assorted clothes hanging there. Such things might be soft to touch, promising the comfort and security of this world. Yet you sense there is more. Rise to the challenge of looking beyond the coats: go beyond the back of the wardrobe. What do you see, smell, touch or feel? Take time to explore this new world imaginatively, using all your senses.

If this feels too fanciful, remember that millions of people struggle to believe in any living world beyond our own. Of course, Narnia isn't heaven, at least not when Lucy and the other children first enter it. They soon learn that it's a world trapped by dark forces: full of 'spies' who serve the Witch who has denied liberty to all Narnia's creatures.

Similarly we live in a 'corrupted' world, but God promises better things to come. We don't know exactly how it will happen or what shape heaven on earth will take when our rightful ruler resumes loving control. Still we pray 'thy kingdom come on earth as it is in heaven'. Spend a few moments repeating these words, handing over to God any obstacles to that belief. Ask that he might flash more glimpses of heaven in our hearts as well as into our world.

Always winter, never Christmas

Reflective

Lucy first enters the wardrobe out of curiosity. She finds fur coats, which she might have expected, then touches snow and prickly, rough branches of trees.

If you can, recall your first experiences of going to church, or of exploring the Christian faith in more depth. Did it feel like entering a different world? If you've no memory of life without church, chat to others who came to faith later in life, or read testimonials on the internet.

Lucy finds it both exciting and frightening to leave her own world of summer and familiar people. When travelling in our world, we are likely to observe many differences between countries. However, entering a completely different world, in this case a land of talking animals, is something else! Befriending Mr Tumnus, the faun, Lucy learns that Narnia has been trapped by Queen Jadis's spell. It's been winter there for 100 years. For most children, winter's coming spells excitement: it's not long till Christmas! Perhaps you still anticipate Christmas eagerly. But for many older people, particularly the house-bound or homeless, winter is an endlessly dark, dreary season. Similarly, some adults think attending church or following the Christian faith is an uncomfortable, even dull experience. Maybe this accounts for the millions who only attend church on special festivals, like Christmas, when the format of readings and carols is familiar and colourful.

Consider how newcomers might find church services. Next time you go to church, walk in with the eyes of a newcomer and imagine Jesus beside you. How does it feel as you stand there with Jesus? What are the strengths/weaknesses of what's going on? Determine to do at least one thing the following Sunday which might help a newcomer feel more comfortable.

Turkish delight

Bible study

Read Romans 7:4–25.

Edmund's experience of entering Narnia contrasts sharply with Lucy's. His first encounter is with the White Witch, who fiercely challenges his coming into 'her' kingdom. As readers, we quickly realise Jadis is no ordinary queen, but a villain who adapts her behaviour towards Edmund once realising his usefulness to her. She pretends to be interested in meeting all four children. Diverting them away from fulfilling Aslan's prophecy will maintain her rule. Using flattery and deceit, Jadis lures Edmund into her service, notably offering him endless supplies of his favourite food, Turkish delight (see how Paul describes such behaviour in 2 Corinthians 11:13–15).

Like Adam and Eve tempted by the serpent in the garden of Eden, Edmund longs for self-sufficiency and instant gratification. Before long, he questions Aslan's authority and good intentions. Similar selfishness can make us deny God's power over our lives.

Without getting too serious or hung up about any personal 'addictive' behaviours, are there any patterns that have lured you away from following God's leading in the past, or from doing so now? We're all prey to one or more of the seven deadly sins: pride, greed, lust, envy, gluttony, wrath and sloth.

In Edmund's case, gluttony isn't the only sin that drives him further into the queen's service. More subtle promptings guide him too, such as deception – thinking something was good for him when it wasn't. Many Christians get tricked into believing they're serving God when they're actually serving self-interest.

Read the Bible passage again. Paul's explanation about God's grace negating the effects of sin is quite complex. Remember too Hebrews 2:18: 'Because he himself [Jesus] was tested by what he suffered, he is able to help those who are being tested.' Hopefully this will aid your handing over of any temptations to God. End your time by making a symbolic gesture of this; that is, if greedy, skip a treat and give its cost to charity, or draw anything that makes you angry/envious/lazy, then pray with that image.

How could it be true?

Intercession

When Lucy first returns from Narnia, she joyfully relates her adventure to Peter, Susan and Edmund. They can't make sense of it: no time has passed since she left, plus they find only coats in the wardrobe. So logic dictates that either Lucy is mad or she's not telling the truth. Lucy's excitement returns on discovering that Edmund has been to Narnia too. His testimony will finally back up her story! Unfortunately, her optimism is misplaced: Edmund lies, insisting Lucy is playing games and that Narnia 'is all nonsense'.

Peter and Susan wisely decide to ask the Professor about the wardrobe. He poses an unexpected theory: if Lucy hasn't shown a propensity towards madness before, and is generally more honest than Edmund, why shouldn't her story be true?

Many of us struggle to explain the validity of our faith to others. We probably all know people who think belief in God and heaven is just 'fanciful', based on illogical hopes and fears. I suspect Lewis thought that when beliefs harden like this, it's like living in Narnia under the Witch's spell: the world always seems gripped by winter, never turning to spring. Yet when Peter, Susan and Lucy leave the Beaver family home to seek out Aslan and their lost brother, the world around them starts to thaw, proving that spring comes in the most unlikely places!

Create a list of people you know who are agnostic or even atheist. Now add another column for people you're not sure about. Pray for ways to challenge their 'logic' or disinterest. Ask that they be thawed out by the Spirit's power. Your own testimony might be a factor, but it's more likely to be their own awakened sense of wonder that opens them up to light. Pray consistently for them in the coming days, asking for God's new life to penetrate any brittle resistance.

Not a tame lion

Creative

Even non-cat-lovers probably recognise the awesome beauty of lions. Though fearsome creatures to their prey, they're impressively protective of their young. Living in groups called prides, lions once roamed most of Africa and parts of Asia and Europe. They were hunted or driven out of much of their natural terrain. Today, only parts of sub-Saharan Africa are home to them, though there's a small population of Asian lions living in India's Gir Forest.

Apparently, Lewis chose to depict his hero creature, Aslan, as a lion because he came 'bounding in' to his imagination. After that, it seems the stories almost wrote themselves with Aslan's direction.

In *The Lion, the Witch and the Wardrobe*, Lewis cleverly resists revealing Aslan's physical nature too quickly. On hearing his name for the first time, the children's reactions are telling. Edmund feels 'a sensation of mysterious horror'; Peter is stirred to feel 'brave and adventurous'. Susan senses that 'a delightful strain of music has just floated by her'. For Lucy, Aslan's name evokes great excitement like waking up to discover the summer holidays have started.

All four children expect the true ruler of Narnia to be a compliant, easy-going creature: a kind of 'gentle Jesus, meek and mild'. This assumption is quickly challenged. Once we see Aslan in action, we learn that his goodness, like that of our God, knows no compromises. His love can sometimes be tough and cannot be tamed to human expectations.

Create a collage from images/fabrics that suggest the 'lion-like' qualities of God. A lion's face has affinity with the sun; that glorious golden mane tempts the children to stroke Aslan. Once you've finished, pray over Aslan's links with Jesus the Son, adapting this prayer to mirror your own sense of God's 'wild' nature:

Father God, thank you for being more awesome than Aslan, in your loving nature and actions. You are majestic, courageous and boldly desire to defend us, your children, when dark powers strike. Yet you are so much more…

Help me in times when I struggle to comprehend your 'wildness'. Sovereign God, help me to consciously give back to you things I find unexpected, even 'shocking', about you and your perceived plans for me.

Help me to daily release control over to you, to trust and celebrate as I go deeper into the adventure of new life. May your Spirit prompt me to set aside fears and prejudices: everything I know and value, when it is not of your kingdom. Amen

Preparing for battle

Bible study/creative

Read:

- 2 Chronicles 20:1–18
- Ephesians 6:10–18
- 2 Corinthians 10:1–7

Recently I visited the modern town of Sparta in Greece. Near the ruins of this ancient city-state stands an impressive black statue of a warrior king. Leonidas I led his forces to a last stand against the invading Persian army in the fifth century BC.

I suspect Leonidas's heavy battle armour was very different from that given to the children in *The Lion, the Witch and the Wardrobe*. In the story, Father Christmas calls these weapons 'tools', suggesting that battles come in all shapes and sizes, not just open warfare. He warns of external crises where the children will face darkness head on, but also of inner struggles that have as yet gone unrecognised.

In his letter to the Ephesians, Paul looks at the power God gives us to fight *all* types of evil. The armour he talks of is mostly protective, giving powers of discernment and renewal rather than aggression. Regardless of belief in an actual devil, few Christians question that spiritual warfare is rampant in our world. The reading from 2 Chronicles reminds us of the need to be ready 'for battle', giving prayerful trust to God even if we don't personally participate in external conflict. Lewis explores this when he comments about the girls, Susan and Lucy, not being meant to fight.

Read the Bible passages again, then list the 'weapons' God has provided for you. How have you used these in life so far? How might you need their defending power in future? Finish by drawing the weaponry described in Ephesians. Label each item to suggest what it represents for you, asking for God's protective power to envelop you at all times.

Deep magic

Imaginative

Christ's atonement for our sins was intended to return humanity to God's original plan, as depicted in the garden of Eden, hence the human characters in *The Lion, the Witch and the Wardrobe* are called 'sons of Adam' and 'daughters of Eve'. However, God's redemption never comes via 'manipulation of forces' which is what normal magic involves.

Unlike the Witch, Aslan refuses to distort truth or promise more than he can righteously deliver. Likewise, our all-sovereign God, in total love, refuses to be a magician or compromise human free will. Often we're reminded that the ability to choose to reject God has its consequences. We may suffer the effects of evil in our world, while being innocent of creating that specific evil.

Likewise, when faced with defending our faith, many Christians 'feel alone' on earth. There are no easy shortcuts, only Christ's vital promise of final judgement and mercy that will ultimately right all wrongs. In the meantime, we can praise God for kick-starting this process: for sending his son to redeem us through his life, death and resurrection. The Spirit's mighty power was released for all earthly children to claim.

In Lewis's story, Aslan is the redeemer who takes Edmund's place when the Witch demands the wayward boy as her sacrifice. Susan and Lucy, like the disciples during the last days of Christ, don't know what's going on during this enormous cosmic battle between good and evil. As in the Bible's telling of events in the garden of Gethsemane, the girls sense the terrible dark force bearing down on Aslan before he is tied up. Later, like the two Marys standing at the cross of Jesus, they feel powerless. When Aslan is slaughtered by the Witch, it appears that all hope is gone.

If you can, read the dramatised part of Mark's Passion narrative at **www.oremus.org/liturgy/lhwe/mark.html**, or alternatively, read Mark chapters 14 and 15. Try to imagine yourself as a character standing at the cross. Sense the struggle Christ had in handing himself over to worldly forces, while knowing that future human destiny hinged on his actions. Can you sense what that felt like? What is your response – either as a character watching him suffer, or as yourself? Do you want to draw closer to Christ, perhaps hug his feet if you can reach them? Or maybe cry out in anger, even attack the people enjoying this spectacle? What is your dominant emotion?

Whatever your response, offer it to Jesus, knowing that he understands. Thank him for forgiving the worst things humanity can hurl at him.

Breathing new life

Going out

Read Romans 8:18–39.

On coming back to life, Aslan roars and runs around playfully with the children. As children reveal when they play, transformation and rebirth should be fun! So after overcoming the Witch and her forces, Aslan breathes new life into those previously turned to stone for daring to confront that evil power. The children marvel at seeing a multitude of creatures, including a 'stone lion' and Lucy's old friend Mr Tumnus, come to life again under the power of Narnia's true king.

Go outside and look for signs of winter turning into spring. As you breathe out, it might be cold enough for you to see your own breath. Imagine this breath as God's power, 'breathing out' new life everywhere. Smile with each new inward breath. Visualise it as God's never-ending gift of life to you. Then pass on each outward breath to the world and its people.

Imagine breathing out new life as you pass any sad/oppressed faces in the street. If you encounter positive signs of growth in nature or receive a smile from others, thank God for signs of transforming life. Use these words from Psalm 150:6: 'Let everything that breathes praise the Lord! Praise the Lord!'

Kings and queens

Creative

At the end of *The Lion, the Witch and the Wardrobe*, Peter, Susan, Edmund and Lucy become kings and queens of Narnia. Even without Aslan's presence, they remain wise and caring sovereigns for many years.

Find pictures or written accounts of sovereigns, past and present. Add world or church leaders to these. Write a brief description or paste pictures of them on to your 'lion' collage (see p. 25). Then add a 'tick' or a 'cross' next to each to indicate your sense of whether they've used power positively or negatively.

Compare and contrast these with the 'lion' images you've already assembled. Do you have a clearer picture now of Christ, the ultimate ruler of our world and the world to come – Christ, the servant king and Christ the king, sitting at the right hand of the Father? The only human ruler who 'gave all', loving and serving everyone without discrimination.

Take a pack of cards. Extract the kings and queens. Use these to help you think about royalty or other leadership down the ages. Black cards could symbolise those who ruled well and the red represent those who abused or over-extended their power. Now pick out the jacks, or knaves as they are sometimes called, and also the jokers in the pack. Have fun using your imagination to think of leaders who fall into these categories!

Finish by thinking about our own royal family. The media has been keen to show their ups and downs over the years. We, in our 'royal' position as part of the Christian family, can likewise promote positive or negative images in attempts to be salt and light to the world. So it's a relief to know that whatever we do, Christ is the ace in the pack. He's able to trump the poor cards we play.

Pray for all rulers, especially those struggling to maintain justice and peace. Ask for the Prince of Peace to guide them and those surrounding them today.

Aslan in our world

Imaginative/going out

As kings and queens of Narnia, Peter, Susan, Lucy and Edmund ultimately decide to hunt the White Hart. The creature leads them back into the wardrobe, into their own world, where time has stood still.

After years leading a different life, they don't know what to make of it all. Wisely they ask the Professor's advice again: he seems unsurprised by such strange happenings but cautions them against telling others of their adventures. Lewis suggests here that we too should be circumspect before openly evangelising about our faith. We must always seek the Spirit's lead, particularly if we sense any resistance due to previous negative experiences. Spend time thinking more about how Aslan in Lewis's story is like Jesus coming into our world. For some, Jesus is immediately attractive, a saviour and a friend. For others, he's an intriguing healer or just a fascinating person from human history. Sceptics may think him just a myth; like gods and goddesses from ancient times, only worshipped by primitive people.

The reality of God can be missed if we make him too big or remote, beyond human understanding. If made too small, he can't be seen in all sorts of people and places. C.S. Lewis encouraged people to be emotionally challenged, to look beyond what's seen as 'fact' or 'proof'. Human nature can distort truth and is prone to reject all beyond our immediate comprehension. But with God's help, we can keep expanding our vision, keep open to fresh possibilities.

In the days ahead, note and give thanks when you sense that 'Aslan is on the move'. It might be in a particular situation, where movement could go almost unrecognised. One way to actively seek out that movement could be looking at recently answered prayer. Lewis ends his adventure story with the Professor promising that Narnia will 'happen when you're not looking for it'. Thank God when you receive one of these unexpected blessings.

Parables

Joy MacCormick

Parables

Introduction

As a child I was taught that 'a parable is an earthly story with a heavenly meaning'. True enough as far as it goes, but it tends to overlook the very practical, down-to-earth messages for daily living and relationships which many parables contain.

Another definition often offered is that a parable is a story with an unexpected twist, or even a sting in its tail. Frequent repetition of most parables has led to them becoming so familiar that we no longer notice any twist or sting. Familiarity does indeed breed contempt – or at least complacency.

In addition, many of us have been provided with 'the meaning' of parables – implying that there is only one way for each story to be understood. No room is left for exploring it to discover any new or different treasure it might contain. This, of course, has been going on ever since the Gospels were first written down. In fact it is probably a direct consequence of the transition from oral transmission (which always allowed for, and often included, variation) to the fixed immutability of the written word and the concern for uniformity and orthodoxy as the institutional church developed. Some people believe that when the meaning of a parable is placed on the lips of Jesus, it is more likely to have been added by the writer at a later date.

In their original Aramaic language and Middle Eastern culture, stories contained multiple meanings and the 'correct' one was that which touched the individual on any particular day. Thus the meaning could be different for different individuals, or differ for the same person from one day to another.

In this section I will offer some different ways to look at familiar stories, focusing on the sower and on images of God and the kingdom of heaven. None of these interpretations is definitive any more than the received or familiar ones are. I invite you to enter them with a sense of exploration and anticipated discovery. As you work through the parable of the sower, you might like to plant some seeds and tend them and watch them grow. You can then nurture to full growth, or give them away for others to nurture.

Read the story of the sower (Mark 4:1–9), then prayerfully open yourself to the presence of the Spirit to lead you on a hunt for treasure buried in familiar earth. With what do you need to be equipped? What do you need to leave behind?

The sower – pathways

Imaginative

> *A sower went out to sow. And as he sowed, some seed fell on the path, and the birds came and ate it up.*
>
> MARK 4:3–4

Imagine yourself standing at the edge of recently ploughed land. Notice the general contour – is it sloping, flat or undulating? Notice the colour of the soil, the ridges and furrows, the way the sun strikes them, the birds flying above and dropping down to find nourishment. Feel the openness, the lack of restriction, the unlimited possibility of the tilled earth.

Now visualise the same scene with a well-trodden path leading across it. What feelings and thoughts arise as you see this? What purpose does such a pathway serve?

Reflect on this as an image of your life. What, figuratively, are the well-trodden pathways which get you quickly, easily and without thought from one place to another? Those ingrained, automatic, instinctive reactions (thoughts, words or deeds) in unguarded moments, which limit fullness of humanity – your own or that of others? When are you likely to act without thinking? Do you have a dismissive attitude, a tendency to rigidity of opinion, or...?

While these 'well-trodden pathways' have their purpose, especially in emergencies when speed is of the essence, they may also have become hardened surfaces impermeable to life-bearing seed.

Invite God's gentle refreshing rain to soften any such areas of your life. Feel the drops begin to fall and relax into the experience of becoming more fruitful.

Rocky ground

Reflective

Other seed fell on rocky ground, where it did not have much soil, and it sprang up quickly, since it had no depth of soil. And when the sun rose, it was scorched; and since it had no root, it withered away.

MARK 4:5–6

On the surface this is apparently fertile soil – the rock lies hidden beneath. Seed falling here initially sprouts but its emerging roots soon encounter resistance, the rock is impenetrable, and the scorching heat of the sun withers the young tender plant. It is tempting to view this underlying stone negatively but it does serve a positive purpose. Bedrock is what gives the land its contours, structure and identity. The surface soil may comprise largely weathered rock – rock broken down into soil by the effects of wind, rain and sun. It is in a process of transformation. Are you?

Can you identify times when your initial response to some new idea, some new way of looking at things, even some new concept of God, has been enthusiastic – only for it to wither and die? What caused this? Was it the scorching scorn of others as you shared your new insight? Was it the underlying stone of previous teaching, established beliefs and practices, culture and tradition? You may be able to identify other influences.

Invite the wind, water and fire of the Holy Spirit to work on any rock-like areas in your life which need to be softened and broken down so you can receive what God has in store for you – and for the world through you.

Thorns

Going out

> *Other seed fell among thorns, and the thorns grew up and choked it, and it yielded no grain.*
> MARK 4:7

Thorny plants are often regarded as a nuisance or even despised. Yet they, too, are part of God's creation and their thorns are God's provision. Some even bear nourishing fruit.

Go out and collect a twig from a thorny plant. It might be a blackberry, rose or gorse. Notice which you choose and what influences your choice. Why does it have thorns? What purpose do they serve? What is it like to be this plant? How do you feel about your thorns?

How does your plant reflect the reality of your life and personality? (As it has been, is now or as you might prefer it to be.) When do you become 'prickly'? What self-protective devices do you use and what caused you to develop (need) your 'thorns'? Are they still needed? (Remember that 'Yes' can be as valid a response as 'No'.) Some, but only some, thorny plants, once they reach their mature height or form, no longer grow new thorns. What does this suggest for your own growth?

For many years I have kept a knitted toy hedgehog (acquired at a time when life was difficult and I was responding abrasively to those who sought to help me) where I can see and touch it each day. It is a constant reminder that it is possible to retain one's identity – even as a hedgehog – without being constantly prickly. Keep your prickly twig somewhere where you can see it regularly as a reminder.

Rest for a time in God's presence, giving thanks for God's provision, including the 'thorns' which have protected you in times of need. If you are unsure how necessary their protection is now, ask to be shown. If no longer needed, give thanks for all they have done for you and prayerfully bid them farewell. If they still have a positive purpose to serve, give thanks for their continuing presence and protection and ask how you can grow beyond the need for them.

Good soil

Creative

Other seed fell into good soil and brought forth grain, growing up and increasing and yielding thirty and sixty and a hundredfold.

MARK 4:8

Spend some time reflecting on times when you have known yourself as 'good soil' – receptive to God's word; when you have experienced it taking root deep in your being. What kind of harvest did it produce – in terms of your own life; in terms of nurturing others? Give thanks for this experience – whether a single event or often repeated.

What produces good soil?

While it is part of God's creation, often made through processes such as weathering rock and incorporating decaying plant and animal matter so that death becomes a source of new life, human action can also contribute to good soil, gathering and removing stones, tilling the soil to aerate it and break up hard surfaces, adding compost and manure (yes, all that smelly, rotting stuff).

An old Jewish tradition teaches that God dispenses blessings from both hands. From the right hand flow the blessings we enjoy; from the left, those blessings which we often fail to recognise and struggle to accept. Can you recognise how difficult or painful experiences, trials and tribulations have contributed to enriching the soil of your life and rendering it more fruitful?

I have a friend who has, for many years, suffered from constant severe migraine. She now says that this experience has grown in her a deep compassion for the suffering of others and eventually become a valued source of her ministry.

Spend some time reflecting on and thanking God for those unsought and unwanted blessings which have contributed to enriching the good soil of your life. Draw round your hands. Add the blessings you enjoy to one hand and those you may not have previously recognised or which you might be struggling to accept on the other hand.

Self as sower

Creative

A sower went out to sow.

MARK 4:3

Passing through the crowd of people, the traveller did not see the seeds which trickled through the unnoticed hole in her pack and attached themselves to all with whom she came in contact. The recipients were equally unaware until the seeds germinated and began to grow. Some remained unaware. Others (more alert perhaps) did notice and realised they could root out the invasive plant if they so chose, or let it grow and then reap the harvest – whatever that might be.

It was a crucial decision, for the nature of the plant was often obscure. Would it produce compassion, forgiveness, love or healing? Would it produce resentment, anger, bitterness or division?

Only time would tell.

Have you ever seen yourself as a sower of seeds? How does it feel to sow and nurture seeds? If you haven't already, try planting some seeds.

Even though we are usually oblivious to the fact, all of us sow seeds every day as we pass through life. By our words and deeds, by our very demeanour, we scatter seeds which may take root and grow – we know not where or in whom. Some of the seeds we sow will be nourishing and life-giving; others may be invasive corrosive weeds. Only by becoming conscious of ourselves as sowers can we begin to take responsibility for which seeds we sow.

Take time in God's presence to reflect on seeds which have been sown in you and have brought forth pain or struggle; maybe even death of dreams or relationships. Offer to God any pain or resentment you still bear. Pray for healing for yourself and those you see as responsible for the hurt.

Now consider those seeds which have borne fruit, nourishing yourself and others. Give thanks and find a way to celebrate what you have contributed. You may like to write your own Magnificat in celebration, based on Mary's from Luke 1:46–55.

Old ideas and new

Creative

> *Do not be conformed to this world, but be transformed by the renewing of your minds, so that you may discern what is the will of God – what is good and acceptable and perfect.*
>
> ROMANS 12:2

Challenges to received wisdom and traditional practice are seldom welcomed – especially by those who are in authority or who are secure in the status quo. The stories Jesus told about the nature of God and God's kingdom were often quite revolutionary and offensive to such as these, although welcomed by the poor and the oppressed. Those who believed themselves to be safe as residents of a kingdom which promised rich rewards for observing every detail of the religious law, the Torah, had little reason to welcome an itinerant teller of such disturbing tales.

What is your initial reaction when one of your cherished beliefs about God or the church is challenged? Do you feel defensive, curious, confused, angry, excited or… ? If your feeling had a colour what would it be? What shape might it assume? On paper draw or doodle your response – preferably with your non-dominant hand (left if you are right-handed, right if you are left-handed). Add colour if possible. When you have finished, close your eyes for a few minutes and ask the Holy Spirit to guide your thoughts and feelings as you open your eyes and look at what you have produced. What do you see? What does this suggest about how open you are to new ideas about God and God's kingdom? Journal these responses and offer them prayerfully to God.

The lost sheep

Imaginative

> *Which one of you, having a hundred sheep and losing one of them, does not leave the ninety-nine in the wilderness and go after the one that is lost until he finds it?*
>
> LUKE 15:4

Slowly and carefully read the full story in Luke 15:1–7. (You can also read this parable in Matthew 18:12–14.)

A familiar, comfortable and reassuring tale as we receive it – but in its original setting and directed, as it was, to those who regarded themselves as leaders in all things godly (vv. 2–3), it would have been highly offensive, while no doubt treasured by the tax collectors and sinners who were listening.

Since at least the time of David, the image of God as 'Shepherd of Israel' had been part of Jewish tradition – just think of Psalm 23 or many other Old Testament references. By Jesus' day shepherds were no longer so highly regarded. The nature of their work meant they were unable to participate in the religious rituals so were often regarded as unclean. For those who valued their religious purity, to be equated with shepherds would be grossly insulting. The suggestion that God might value a sinner as highly as the righteous would be seen as nigh on blasphemy. Of course, in reality, a shepherd would not abandon his flock like this, so what was Jesus seeking to accomplish by this exaggeration?

Either In a quiet place and time imagine yourself among those listening to Jesus. Who are you? What have you been taught about God and the kingdom – and how you fit in? Read the story as if you were listening to it for the first time. How does this story challenge your beliefs? How do you feel?

How do your current beliefs and behaviour fit with the story?

Does anything need to change? Bring this to a conversation with Jesus.

Or Imagine yourself as the lost sheep being returned to the flock. What happens? How are you received? Notice your feelings at different stages in the story. Journal the story of your adventure.

The lost coin

Reflective

> *Or what woman having ten silver coins, if she loses one of them, does not light a lamp, sweep the house, and search carefully until she finds it?*
>
> LUKE 15:8

Tucked between the parables of the lost sheep and the lost son, the significance of this short (three verse) story is easily overlooked. Take a few moments to read it in full (Luke 15:8–10). What, for you, are the significant features?

Like the two other stories, it portrays God searching for that which is lost and rejoicing when it is found, but its true significance lies in where it differs from the other two parables. Both the sheep and the son were able, had they so chosen, to avoid becoming lost. The coin, being inanimate, had no such option – nor could it contribute to the likelihood of its being found. We are told that it was lost inside the house; what might this 'house' represent? Is there any significance in the house being dark? And if the seeker in those other stories is God, who is God in this story? Does your language for God reflect this?

Have a conversation with Jesus about his use of this image and your response to it.

The lost son

Poetry

Jesus said, 'There was a man who had two sons.'

LUKE 15:11

Read Luke 15:11–32 as if for the first time, with no preconceptions, and be alert to anything which catches your attention or surprises you. The three characters could each represent a part of yourself. What are they? To which one do you most easily relate? Why?

Most of us are able to recognise aspects of each of both sons within ourselves, but what about the father? What do you know of how he may have felt seeing his younger son go astray and longing for his return; or seeing his elder son, outwardly dutifully obedient but inwardly resentful and rebellious, unwilling or unable to join in the family celebration or even to take his place among the family?

When we ache for those who endure suffering, or those who (knowingly or unknowingly) inflict it, are we sharing in the aching father-heart of God who wills all to know healing and wholeness? I wrote the following lines at a time of such pain.

Heartbreak

It breaks my heart
to see you break, repeatedly,
the hearts of others;

casting aside,
like dirty clothing
on the bathroom floor,
those who have dared
to love you.

This sword
that pierces deep into my heart
demands of me
a greater sacrifice of love
than I know how to give.

Then I remember
your own deep brokenness.
Love and compassion flow
and I dare celebrate
the vision of your wholeness.

I hold you, yet again,
with all those other wounded ones
in my own breaking heart.

Hold in your heart before God people and situations for whom your heart aches, and feel God's love reaching out to enfold you and them, bringing the promise of healing and reconciliation.

The mustard seed

Story

> *[Jesus] said therefore, 'What is the kingdom of God like? And to what should I compare it? It is like a mustard seed that someone took and sowed in the garden; it grew and became a tree, and the birds of the air made nests in its branches.'*
>
> LUKE 13:18–19

The garden, surrounded by its protective walls, was a picture of affluence and order. Grape vines, olive and fig trees, pomegranates and even date palms flourished and bore perfect fruit – undamaged by the predations of birds or other pests which were kept away by the army of servants dedicated to that purpose.

None of the ordinary village folk had actually seen the garden – the guard at the gate made sure of that, allowing in only invited guests. The villagers knew about it only from the stories they had heard but it was, in their minds, the very garden of Eden recreated.

Then came 'the weed'!

Today the place hardly warranted the name 'garden', overrun as it was by a rampant invasive weed. Traces of the fruit trees could still be seen but the walls had long since fallen into disrepair and anyone could wander in at any time. Stray animals and other pests joined the birds in making it their home and dining on what fruit they could find, as did many of the outcasts from village society. It was a place where all and any could find shelter, though it was shunned by those pillars of society who had been its former visitors. They dared not risk being made unclean by contact with its present inhabitants.

The strange thing was (so rumour had it) that the landowner himself had planted the weed.

A Jewish friend who has lived in Israel says that the mustard seed referred to in the parable is actually a rampant invasive weed – the last thing one would want in a garden. What plant sprang to mind as you read the story?

Why would Jesus liken the kingdom of God to such a seed? What was he trying to say?

Do you want to be part of this kind of kingdom? Be honest with God about your answer and listen for God's response. Journal your experience.

Yeast in the dough

Creative

> *And again he said, 'To what should I compare the kingdom of God? It is like yeast that a woman took and mixed in with three measures of flour until all of it was leavened.'*
>
> LUKE 13:20–21

Or, in the King James Version, 'Whereunto shall I liken the kingdom of God? It is like leaven, which a woman took and hid in three measures of meal, till the whole was leavened.'

The impact of this little story is diminished by translation into modern English. The word 'yeast' tends to imply a clean, dry granular substance. In Jesus' day nothing like this was available. 'Leaven' was fermented dough, retained from the previous baking and used to produce fermentation in the new batch. Moist, sticky and active, it affects everything with which it comes in contact, and because of its fermented nature was often regarded as unclean. Hence the Passover ritual of removing every trace of leaven from the house (see Exodus 12:19). Jesus also warns his followers to 'beware of the yeast [leaven] of the Pharisees, that is, their hypocrisy' (Luke 12:1). Yet he uses leaven as a symbol of the kingdom of God! Why might this be?

In the King James Version Jesus says the woman hid the leaven in the meal. What does this add to the story? Where, how and why might the kingdom be hidden? What is your experience of this?

Get some fresh yeast and add sugar and water and leave it in a warm place as you watch it rise. This also works with dried yeast. Smell the yeast as it ferments.

Does this story (and the previous one) challenge your concept of the kingdom? In what ways? Hold this in prayer and be open to what God shows you.

Being with God through creativity

Jean Sims

Creator God

Introduction

Each one of us is made in an image of our creator God; therefore, whether we feel it or not, we each have a spark of that creativity within us, waiting to be set alight. There are endless ways of being creative, such as music, movement, gardening, woodworking, cooking, sewing, writing, designing, building, clearing away litter, nurturing a friendship, bringing up a child, dying a 'good death', and so much more.

In this section the focus is on a selection of ways to use our hands to make and create with art materials, but also using mind and heart to reflect, feel and respond. Some of the suggestions are directed, while some are more about starting with an idea and then seeing what happens and where God takes us.

You will not be attempting to create a perfect product. It is the doing, making, exploring and experimenting which is important. It may well turn out to be a worthwhile struggle, or deeply satisfying. Each time, when you feel that it is nearly time to stop, allow a few minutes to reflect, with God, on what you have been doing.

Honour what you have made by not destroying it straight away, but returning to look at it later. In creating it, it has been part of you.

Over these creative days you might like to put together a prayer space or corner using what you have made, honouring God's gift to you. All the time, try to remember that God is with you in this, he is enjoying being with you, in the making and in what you have made, in the creating and in the creation. Being with God in this is one way of allowing our creator closer to us to continue to create us and to create in us, as one way of answering this prayer:

Create in me a pure heart, O God, and renew a steadfast spirit within me.

PSALM 51:10

Making a praise spiral

Creative

You will need: paper or thin card; a circular plate; scissors; coloured pens or pencils; a length of thread, string or wool

Place the plate on the paper and draw round it.

Cut out the circle.

Starting from the outside edge, cut into the circle in a spiral. (If you do not feel confident about this, you could draw the spiral before you cut.)

On the spiral write some sentences or words praising God.

They will look more attractive if you use coloured pens or pencils. You may choose colours that suggest praise to you.

You might want to use your own words, or phrases from the Bible, or from hymns, or modern worship songs. Here are some suggestions to get you started:

Holy, holy, holy is the Lord Almighty.
ISAIAH 6:3

Let us sing for joy to the Lord; let us shout aloud to the Rock of our salvation.
PSALM 95:1

To our God and Father be glory for ever and ever.
PHILIPPIANS 4:20

Great and marvellous are your deeds,
Lord God Almighty.
Just and true are your ways,
King of the nations.
REVELATION 15:3

Now make a small hole in the centre of the spiral and tie thread through it, so that you can hold the thread and allow the spiral to move freely. As you watch it move, remember and use the words you have written. Say them silently, or out loud, or sing them to praise God. Is there somewhere you can hang your mobile?

A zigzag book of names of Jesus

Creative

You will need: a piece of paper A4 size; scissors; sticky tape; felt-tip pens or coloured pencils

Cut the paper in half, so that you have two long, narrow strips of paper. Fold each piece into three, to make three approximate squares. Then open out the paper.

Use adhesive tape to join the two strips of paper together on a short side and fold on the join.

Now adjust the folds so that you have a zigzag book.

Jesus has many names, each of which says something about his character, or about how we best relate to him at different times in our lives, or moods, or circumstances. It can be enriching and humbling to use a particular name of Jesus at different stages of our relationship with him; remembering these names can help us look back and see where he has been in our lives, and where he is now.

On each page of your book write one of the many names given to Jesus. You could use coloured pencils or pens. Maybe you want to draw on, or decorate, each page with colours, or images, which relate to the particular name.

Start by using names which are, or have been, significant for you.

There are some suggestions below which you could choose from as well as using your own ideas.

Friend	Saviour	Master	Suffering Servant
Lord	Lover	Emmanuel	Son of God
Companion	Redeemer	High Priest	Prince of Peace
Good Shepherd	Messiah	Bread of Life	Living Water
Word of Life	Teacher	King of Kings	Anointed One
Light of the World	Healer	Deliverer	Lamb of God

Your book will be compact enough to keep with you in a pocket or bag, so that you can use it prayerfully wherever you are. If you have a prayer corner, or prayer space, it could stand there to be used over and over again.

Praying the news

Creative/intercession

You will need: an up-to-date newspaper; scissors; a sheet of paper or card, A3 size or larger; glue

Offer this time to God. Now look through the newspaper and cut out any pictures, or headlines, which catch your attention. Arrange them on the sheet of paper as a collage. You might like to overlap them to cover the paper, or position them in the shape of the cross. Then stick each one on to the paper. As you do this, pause, ask God to show you what to pray and then pray for each item. If it is difficult to know what to pray, hold each person or situation in the love of God, as you make your collage. Don't forget, there will be people or situations to thank God for, as well. Notice if there is any particular item which seems of especial importance to you; this might mean that God is prompting you to return to it in your prayers in the following days.

Moving colours

Creative

You will need: several pieces of smooth paper; water; diluted water-based paint; decorator's paint brush or large artist's brush; a smaller, soft-haired artist's brush; some protection for the work surface; a drinking straw (optional); a hairdryer (optional)

This is very much a way of playing with the paint and seeing what happens, so relax and be prepared to be surprised.

With the largest brush, cover one of the pieces of paper with water. Before the surface dries, dab or drop brushfuls of paint on to it, so that the colour merges and moves across the paper, seemingly by itself. Take time to watch it move.

If you want to control the movement, gently lift a corner of the paper or, using the drinking straw, get down on a level with the paper and blow the paint in the direction you want.

Try again several times with fresh sheets of paper.

When you have finished, it is best to let the papers dry naturally, but you could use a hairdryer if time is short.

Spend time looking at what you have created from different angles. Is there one that is your particular favourite? Can you say why?

Now reflect on what you have been doing.

Were you happier partially controlling the movement or leaving it alone?

What might this tell you about yourself?

Were there any anxieties or difficulties? Do you know why?

Was there any sense of serendipity or wonder?

Maybe you thoroughly enjoyed yourself.

Share whatever you have discovered with God and, if needed, with some trustworthy person.

If you don't have any paints, try using felt-tip pens or food colouring on wet paper and see what you can create.

Illuminated letters

Creative

You will need: paper; a pencil; a rubber; coloured pencils or pens

Before the invention of printing, when scribes copied the Gospels and other devotional works by hand, they spent time carefully, and often joyfully, creating decorated initial letters in their manuscripts. The colours they used were often costly and rare. These illuminated manuscripts gave glory to God and showed the importance of the text, but the scribe could also use the actual act of decorating as a way into prayer and meditation.

Choose a word to pray with, for example, love, joy, hope, mercy.

With a pencil, lightly outline the word on the paper. Make the initial letter larger than the others and hollow inside. When you are satisfied with the shape, use coloured pens or pencils to write the word, decorating the largest letter with intricate patterns such as whirls, circles, lines or zigzags. If you have any, you can use metallic pens to enhance your work.

As you do this, slowly and thoughtfully repeat the word many times.

With your body comfortable, and leaving aside any concerns which you might have, relax into prayer. Say your word several times out loud, slowly and reverently. Eventually let the word die down inside you until you are with God in silence, savouring his presence.

Praying with a picture

Creative

You will need: a picture. It could be a postcard, or from a magazine, from a book or from the internet. It may be obviously religious, or not so. Allow yourself to be drawn to a picture rather than thinking about the decision.

When you have settled on a picture, give the time to God, asking to be discerning and open to the leading of the Holy Spirit. Ask, 'Please show me.'

You might wish to carry on a conversation with God, remembering to listen, or perhaps be more contemplative in this time.

Spend time looking carefully at your picture.

Why did you choose it? What does it represent, or what is it for you?

What feelings come to the surface as you look at it?

Is there some link with it in a personal way? Does it connect with particular memories?

Perhaps it can be related to scripture, or your prayer life or where God is particularly present in your life at the moment.

Take time to think.

After a time, stop the thinking process and simply look at the picture. Sit with it in God's presence. Become aware of God looking at it with you.

Close your eyes, if this helps, and just be present to your picture and what it has meant to you.

Leave time at the end of your prayer time to review the thoughts and feelings you have had, as a way of discerning where God has been in this time.

Responding to a song, hymn or psalm with paint or pastel

Creative

You will need: a recording (or your memory) or words of a hymn, song or psalm; paper; paint and paint brushes or pastels

Relax and offer the time to God.

Play, sing or read your chosen song, hymn or psalm, listening to the words and the mood of the music.

When you are ready, choose some colours and then start responding with paint or pastel on the paper. Remember, you are not trying for a perfect picture, but seeing what comes. The picture might turn out to be figurative, or more abstract.

When you have finished, spend time looking carefully at your picture from different angles. Remember your thoughts and feelings as you responded to the song. If you have not done so already, have a conversation with God about them, remembering to listen to God's part of the conversation, or just allow God to be with you in your prayerful picture.

If you have used pastels you might want to use a fixative (or hairspray as a cheaper option) to stop it smudging.

Footprints: journeying with Jesus

Creative

You will need: coloured, white or patterned paper or card (you could use a magazine or an old newspaper); pencil or pen; scissors; a camera (optional)

Draw round your right foot and then your left foot and cut out the shapes. Use these templates to draw round and then cut out about ten more pairs of your paper footprints. Now place them on the floor as if they are your actual footprints. If the weather is dry and still, you could do this outside.

Carefully arrange them in various ways to suggest walking in a straight line, or meandering round the space, or suddenly changing direction. You could make them look as if you have been running, or jumping, or wearily dragging your feet. Maybe you have walked round in circles, or in a spiral, or out of sight.

If you wish, take a photo of each arrangement, to look at later.

Imagine that the footprints show different ways in which you have walked with Jesus in your life. Which arrangement shows how you are at the moment? Which show how you have been in the past? Create a pattern that shows how you would like to be.

Do you have any sense of where Jesus might be? Is he ahead of you, walking with you, or carrying you? Is he close to you, or somewhere else? You could add further footprints to show this.

How do you feel about this?

Talk with him about it. How is he responding to you?

Ask him where he would put the footprints.

Playing with pastels as prayer

Creative

You will need: some paper with a slightly rough surface ('tooth'); coloured pastels or chalk (you could use a fixative, or hairspray as a cheaper alternative)

You might be approaching this way of praying with excitement and anticipation, but if you feel apprehensive and that this way of praying is challenging for you, then:

- Let go of the need to produce an end product.
- Let go of the desire to get good results.
- Let go of the urge to compare yourself with others.
- Let go of any fear or apprehension.
- Put all these feelings and baggage into God's keeping.

Start from where you are. Be gentle and patient with yourself. Before you begin, remember to relax and take time to be still, giving the time to God.

Pick some colours and spread them over the paper. Let your hand movements be the way they want to be. They could be quick or slow, or you might vary the speed. They might turn out to be smooth and flowing, or jerky and erratic. You could use your fingers and your hands to blend colours and marks together. Take your time. Eventually, when you are sure that you have finished, you could fix the pastels to stop them rubbing off the paper, or onto anything else, by spraying the paper with fixative or hairspray. It is best to do this outside to avoid breathing in any fumes.

When you are ready, spend time looking carefully at what you have made. Turn the paper around so that you see it from different angles. Accept what you have done without analysing or judging it.

As you sit with it, look back over the time you have spent creating.

What thoughts and feelings did you have as you were using the pastels?

Where was God in all this?

Does it show you anything about yourself or about God?

It could be helpful to write down some of these thoughts, so that you can return to them another time. Remember to keep what you have done for at least a few days, as you might wish to come back to it. If you decide to get rid of it eventually, do that prayerfully too. It has been part of your time with God and deserves respect.

Playing and praying with clay

Creative

You will need: a handful of clay or modelling dough (if you don't have any, look on the internet for a simple recipe for making playdough); a board or piece of thick card, A4 size or larger; a damp cloth; a bowl of water

Place the clay on the board in front of you.

Pray that you will be aware of God and be able to listen with discernment.

Hold the clay in your hands. Feel its weight and texture. Is it cold or warm?

Start to play with the clay, exploring its texture.

Discover more about the clay by manipulating it. Pull it, squash it, smooth it, roll it into a ball or a sausage shape, fold it, coil it. If the clay becomes dry and starts to crack, moisten it with water.

As you play with the clay a shape will emerge. Develop the shape until you feel that it is complete.

Look at it carefully. Does it have any meaning for you? Is there something which needs prayer? Even if you are dissatisfied with it, keep it for a few days, possibly returning to it to sit with it.

Now spend time reflecting on the experience of playing with the clay.

How did you feel as you used it?

Did any memories surface? If they are happy, thank God. If they are painful and need healing, offer them to God and consider sharing them with a wise and trustworthy person.

Did you have any thoughts as you played with the clay?

Bring all these to God.

Creating from junk

Creative

You will need: an old cardboard box, teabag box size or larger; odd scraps of coloured paper, magazines or wrapping paper; scissors; PVA glue; sticky tape; oddments of ribbon, wool, sweet papers, glitter, sequins, etc. (optional); felt-tip pens

Rework the box by cutting into it so that you have a container, with a lid, which will open and close. You may need to use adhesive tape to strengthen the joins on the inside.

Now cover the outside of the box by pasting it over with scraps of coloured paper, making it look as attractive or as quirky as possible. Decorate it with any oddments you might have, or with patterns drawn with coloured pens. Just use what you already have.

Tie it with a ribbon or bow to finish your gift box, if it needs it. This could be made from a strip of paper, if there is no ribbon or wool among your oddments.

Place the transformed box in front of you.

It is empty.

What would you like God to put in the box?

Now think again: what would you *really* want God to put in your box, as God's gift to you?

Ask for it.

If you have made this box towards the end of all these creative days, prayerfully look back over them. Is there anything which has emerged from them, and for which you want to ask God?

Maybe you are aware of some gifts which God is already putting in the box. Then you can give thanks in word, song or movement.

Using nature in prayer

Liz Hoare

The world of nature

Introduction

The Bible is full of nature imagery that describes God and our experience of him. God is like a mother hen gathering her chicks, for example, and his voice is like the sound of many waters. We thirst for God like a deer longing for running streams, and following Jesus requires us to be like a seed planted in the ground, dying in order to live fruitfully.

The world of nature has been seen as second only to the Bible for revealing to us what God is like. Indeed the Bible itself declares that 'The heavens are telling the glory of God; and the firmament proclaims his handiwork' (Psalm 19:1). Using nature in prayer means, at one level, simply joining in with the natural world and glorifying God with our hearts and lives as well as our voices. At another level, using nature can also be a springboard for spiritual growth and change. For example, when the letter of James described the doubter as being like a wave of the sea, driven and tossed by the wind, he wanted his readers to learn to pray their requests to God in faith. Or think of the image of the burning bush that caught the attention of Moses and led to a life-changing encounter with God. Rather than thinking that such things only happen to spiritual giants, ponder the words of Elizabeth Barrett Browning (in *Aurora Leigh*, 1856) that 'Earth's crammed with heaven, And every common bush afire with God; But only he who sees, takes off his shoes.'

It is not surprising that spiritual writers have frequently turned to nature to help them write about spiritual things. Today many of us who live in cities have to work a bit harder to relate to the natural world, but most of us still feel a kinship with plants, a starry sky, birds and animals. They remind us of our place in the universe and they continue to speak of things that transcend our vision and experience.

Don't worry if you do not live in the countryside surrounded by evidence of creation. Many of the most creative ways of using nature to help us to pray stem from noticing the details. A bird on the window ledge, moss on the roof tiles or a weed pushing its way up through the concrete pavement can all speak to us of the grace of God and what it means to follow him today.

Observation and patience

Creative

Read Matthew 6:25–33.

Jesus was a close observer of nature. He had many years of preparation for his ministry when he must have learned to watch the birds of the air and the flowers of the field. This practice gave him a fund of metaphors and illustrations for speaking about his heavenly Father and his coming kingdom. It also taught him to notice people around him and to pause to meet the needs of individuals that others failed to notice were even there. This included a woman bleeding in the crowd as it pressed on him, children being shooed away by irritated disciples and a tax collector sitting at his booth. Others saw a sinner; Jesus saw a potential disciple. When blind Bartimaeus called to him, he stopped and stood still, awaiting him. Observation and patience go together and both are needed if we are to notice signs of the kingdom in our midst today.

Find a single flower and see if you can draw it, noticing the details. Concentrate on what you see rather than on producing a perfect likeness. Or you could take a camera outside and photograph some flowers, again focusing on the details of what you see. Using a camera in this way, like drawing, slows us down and helps us to notice the details. Jesus related the lilies of the field to God's loving care and provision, urging us to trust our heavenly Father and not to worry about material things so much. It's not that he does not care about our basic needs, but that when we become obsessed with them, we have no room left to see God's overarching care of us. Observing close up helps us re-order our world view and turn towards our heavenly Father who delights to give us good things.

Soil

Going out

First read Mark 4:1–9.

This parable came alive for me in a new way when I was staying in the Holy Land for a period of study and our teacher took us outside one morning. As he walked around the grounds of the study centre with us he pointed out the different soils one by one: the path where it was hard and dry and the birds were there looking for food; the rocky ground where slim, weedy seedlings had begun to grow, only to be shrivelled in the hot sun; the thorns with their prickles and nothing else; and finally some good fertile soil where plants were thriving.

In Mark's Gospel, this was the first of the parables that Jesus told. Jesus frequently drew on the natural world for his parables: fishing, grain, fields and seeds. These images would have been familiar to everyone since most people worked the land and all depended on the annual harvest to eat. The familiarity with the basic ingredients of the parables made the twist in the tail all the more startling when it came and that was the point. Jesus taught in parables so that people would wake up and see spiritual truths about God in a new way. It was a way of teaching people that involved them because it demanded a personal response.

If you can, go for a walk where there are fields and see if you can find the different types of soil mentioned in the parable. If you can put your hand in the earth and let it run through your fingers, imagine the fertile soil that enables a rich crop yield to reach harvest. Talk to the Lord about your heart as if it is the soil. Invite him into the hard places, bring to him the temptations that quickly stifle new growth and the obstacles that prevent seeds taking root at depth and offer him your heart as a fertile field for new seeds of faith.

Joining with creation

Creative/going out

Many of the psalms praise God in unison with creation, for example Psalm 104. To use an aspect of nature as a springboard for praise and thanksgiving, walk outside, look at nature pictures (perhaps on a calendar or illustrated book), or look out of your window at the clouds. Then slowly, simply, read the psalm and take time to look at and praise God for all the wonder of the natural world. You might like to write your own psalm using the images that have inspired your praise and thanks and offer this to God.

Season of the soul

Reflective

If someone asked you what season it is in your spirit, what would you reply? 'Seasons of the spirit' is one way of reflecting on how it is with your relationship with God. Some people are able to proclaim boldly, 'It is well with my soul.' In this season, it is high summer when the garden (that is, our spiritual life) is lush and colourful with everything growing abundantly and looking its best. All we want to do is praise God and rejoice.

But it is not always like this. There are times of watching once precious things die and learning to let go. It may be that a way of praying that served us well for a season no longer draws us to God. Perhaps a task that brought great joy and a sense of service to the kingdom is no longer available. This is autumn and it can feel dark and joyless, but in the natural world, unless the leaves fall and the flowers fade, there will not be spring and new growth next year. A fallow time is needed for new life to come forth.

If you are feeling that everything is dormant and bleak, with nothing happening at all, think of a winter scene in a forest. Everything is still, snow may cover all signs of life and it is cold. Winter is a time of resting and waiting, learning to trust and hope. Unless a grain of wheat falls into the ground and dies, said Jesus, it remains just a single grain, 'but if it dies, it bears much fruit' (John 12:24). Psalm 30:5 says: 'Weeping may linger for the night, but joy comes with the morning.'

'Morning' is like the springtime of the year when things wake up and fresh beginnings emerge. Perhaps you have been spiritually in a barren place but there are new signs of life at work in you, new possibilities for service, a new liveliness in prayer and worship. The springtime of the soul when the joy promised in Psalm 30 comes to us is possible at any age. The ebb and flow of life are sometimes, but not always, linked to age and each brings with it new opportunities as well as new challenges to test us. Both will help us to know God more fully if we reach out in trust.

You may like to ponder which season you are in at present and reflect on the characteristics that stand out for you in your relationship with God. Is there anything that you want to thank God for in this season? Anything you need help with to navigate? Any qualities of the season you have not noticed before that yield new insight into God's work in your life?

Trees

Bible reading/creative

Read Psalm 1. This psalm has two striking images taken from nature. The first is that of a tree planted by streams of water and yielding fruit in season. The second is of chaff that the wind blows away. The contrast visually is vivid: picture a sturdy tree beside a handful of chaff blown in the wind. Those delighting in God's word develop the qualities of a healthy tree: deep roots, a strong, straight trunk, with branches growing at intervals and sap flowing through them to nourish the leaves. Then comes fruit in due season. How helpful is this image of spiritual growth to you? What nourishes your faith and helps it to keep growing and be fruitful? The idea of meditating on the word of God day and night (v. 2) implies that what shapes our thinking will also shape our life. What kind of roots have you put down as the foundation of your faith? How do you care for your roots?

If you can observe a mature tree, take some time to do so, noting its features, whatever the season. You might like to take a piece of paper and draw a tree. The artwork doesn't matter; what you need is a tree that represents your own life. What would it look like? Roots – how deep are they? Trunk – is it straight and firm or bent over? Branches – are there lots reaching out to embrace the world? Fruit and leaves – what are the signs of fruitfulness in your life at present? Label your tree and spend some time considering its strengths and weaknesses. Give thanks for where growth is present and ask God to show you how you could enable growth where there are weak spots. Speak to God about the fruit you desire to bear and imagine such fruit growing in abundance as you draw up strength through your roots. The image of a tree suggests that growth takes time. There is a need for patience, attentiveness, the expectation of fruit and a discipline of regular watering and pruning. Is there one practical step you could take to move your desire for fruitfulness towards reality? Tell someone what you have decided to do.

Watering the garden

Prayer

St Teresa of Avila (1515–82) had many struggles in prayer and described it as being like watering a garden. She wrote that all prayer is prompted by the Holy Spirit, but it sometimes seems akin to drawing water from a well and involves considerable effort. At other times, prayer is like watering the garden with a ‘windlass’, a kind of pulley. Effort is involved, but we experience a surge of fresh water into our lives, bringing the joyful presence of Christ. Then there are times when the ‘garden’ of our soul seems to have a stream flowing through it and we rest in its life-giving waters. The best time is when gentle rain falls on the fertile soil. Teresa describes these different ways of watering a garden as stages but most of us find ourselves having a wonderful prayer time one day only to struggle and be distracted the next.

As water is to life, so prayer is to the Christian. Teresa is not setting us up to fail with her picture of prayer. Indeed, she said she often returned to the first stage and, as with any well, it occasionally runs dry and all we can do is wait until God fills it up again. All prayer needs to be centred on Christ, so that, like thirsty ground, our souls may soak up his grace.

Ponder the image of the water and how you experience this when you pray. When have you experienced it as flowing freely, refreshing your soul? Talk to God about your desires concerning prayer and picture clear water flowing freely.

A hazelnut

Imaginative

Julian of Norwich was a remarkable woman who lived as an anchoress in the 14th century. This meant a life of solitude and prayer and the giving of spiritual guidance to those who came seeking. In 1373 Julian had a series of visions during a severe illness, from which she almost died, and she spent the rest of her life reflecting on her 'shewings', as she called them. One of the most famous reflections focused on a hazelnut.

> It was at this time that our Lord showed me spiritually how intimately he loves us… And he showed me more, a little thing, the size of a hazel-nut, on the palm of my hand, round like a ball. I looked at it thoughtfully and wondered, 'What is this?' And the answer came, 'It is all that is made.' I marvelled that it continued to exist and did not suddenly disintegrate; it was so small. And again my mind supplied the answer, 'It exists both now and forever, because God loves it.' In short, everything owes its existence to the love of God.
>
> *Revelations of Divine Love*, 5 (Penguin, 1966), p. 68

Julian looked carefully at a tiny part of creation and pondered its meaning. She went on to explain her findings: 'In this "little thing" I saw three truths. The first is that God made it; the second is that God loves it; and the third is that God sustains it.' We don't have to scale huge mountains or go on a lengthy pilgrimage to meet God in creation. We need only look at the intricacy of frost on a window pane, or hold a piece of fruit in our hand. In your time with God today take something small in your hand like a hazelnut and examine it closely: its texture, shape and colour. What do you notice about it? Does it remind you of anything in the character of God or in your experience of him? Perhaps it brings to mind a verse or passage of scripture. Perhaps its very smallness leads you to reach out in trust to your heavenly Father, conscious of the fragility of creation as well as its strength. Try drawing what you see and in so doing, pay attention to the detail and talk to God about the details in your own life that concern you just now. Remember that we exist because God made us, he loves us and he sustains our being day by day.

The character of God

Spotlight

We rightly think of God as utterly different from ourselves, wholly other and therefore beyond all our attempts to pin him down in words. But God is relational and wants us to know him. He has made himself known in different ways: through nature, through the words of scripture and ultimately through Jesus Christ. Scripture itself sometimes struggles to find words to describe what God is like and frequently draws on the natural world for help. Some of these metaphors are familiar ones that we turn to often. God is our rock (Psalm 18:2), solid and dependable. He is closely associated with clouds, for example when he guided the Israelites through the wilderness (Exodus 14:19) or met with Moses on the mountain (Exodus 19:9) and we are reminded of the awe and mystery that surrounds him. In the New Testament, his Spirit is like a mighty wind (Acts 2:2), reminding us that we cannot control him. One of the most well-known metaphors which shows how closely we are connected to God in Christ is the vine. Jesus said 'I am the vine, you are the branches' (John 15:5).

There are other metaphors, however, that may be less familiar, but they are equally relevant for our understanding of God's nature and his relationship to us. In Deuteronomy 32:11–12, God is likened to a mother eagle: 'As an eagle stirs up its nest, and hovers over its young; as it spreads its wings, takes them up, and bears them aloft on its pinions, the Lord alone guided [Israel].' Some images have a multiplicity of meanings. Hosea 14:5 tells us that God is 'like the dew to Israel'. In a country that does not have rain from April to October, the dew is vital for vegetation to flourish. But dew symbolises refreshing too.

Sometimes one image follows another in rapid succession. Deuteronomy 32 says God is Israel's father who created them (v. 6), but also that he is the 'Rock that bore [them]' (v. 18). These images and many more enrich our understanding of the character of God, and their variety and close proximity defy our attempts to pin God down. In the same way, as we ponder some of the metaphors used in the Bible that focus on our relationship with God, we learn what that relationship means in our daily lives. To take just one example, we are the sheep and he is the shepherd (Psalm 23). You may like to take a favourite metaphor from nature that describes God and do a search on it using a Bible dictionary or concordance. You may also think of other images that you have observed in nature that remind you of an aspect of God's character. Add to your list when you go out walking, watch a nature programme or read an illustrated book or magazine and allow each one to speak to you of God.

A prayer walk

Going out

This is an exercise that uses your five senses to pray as you walk. It isn't about getting from A to B, and sitting on a park bench can be as much a part of it as actually walking. You can do it in the city along a canal, through a park or in a remote wilderness. The important thing is to take time to look around you, look up at the sky, down at the ground and pause to examine whatever catches your eye. Take time to listen to the sounds. Birdsong can often be heard above noisy traffic, the wind howls along narrow streets and rain can be felt on the skin anywhere! What can you see, hear, touch, smell? You could even take a piece of fruit or some nuts with you so you taste something from nature on your walk. You will find yourself moving in and out of prayer as you notice things that spark conversation with God, pause and then move on. You may be filled with awe and wonder, thankfulness and joy. You may also be saddened or angered by humanity's destruction of nature or the lack of creativity in buildings and town centres. Pray in whatever way your walk inspires or moves you. When you get home, notice whether your prayer walk has prompted any future action you feel God is asking you to take.

St Francis

Spotlight

There is growing awareness of the peril that the delicate balance of nature faces, in great part due to human exploitation and abuse of natural resources. Climate change, pollution, the decline of so many species of birds, insects and animals, deforestation: the list is long and it is difficult to know what to do to make a difference. Christians need to make a theological response that leads to living differently, and here both the Bible and the way Christians in the past have lived can help us. The way in which the early Celtic Christians and the followers of St Francis were inspired by the wonders of the natural world have caught the modern imagination. This has helped many Christians not only reconnect with God but also live out the gospel in a way that respects the integrity of creation. St Francis's beautiful hymn 'The Canticle of the Creatures' praises God and all creation. It shows how St Francis saw the whole of creation revealing God, with his presence transfiguring it all. Franciscan spirituality is an incarnational spirituality, where creation is an image and the gift and revelation of God himself and we should expect to meet God in and through the world. 'Praised be you, my Lord, with all your creatures', St Francis wrote in his hymn, with 'creatures' including sun, moon, stars, air, water, fire and earth. These creatures were brothers and sisters and therefore deserving of respect. St Francis's love and respect for nature was an integral part of his wider spirituality which included living simply, with humility and in an attitude of peace, working for justice, witnessing to God's overflowing generosity and joining with all creation in praise and thankfulness. Franciscan spirituality continues to seek to live out these values and live in sustainable ways that respect and care for the environment.

Spend some time praising God for his 'creatures' and thinking about how you can best show respect and care for them.

Using nature

Bible reflection

> *We know that the whole creation has been groaning in labour pains until now; and not only the creation, but we ourselves, who have the first fruits of the Spirit.*
>
> ROMANS 8:22–23

There is a strand of Christianity that sees creation in a negative light, getting in the way of our worship of God, but here Paul includes the created world in his picture of redemption and the new creation. A few verses earlier he describes creation as waiting 'with eager longing' (v. 19), a lovely picture of anticipation. Creation is not to be despised as worthless but as precious to God. One way of understanding the Celtic cross, with its circle, is to see the work of the cross as encompassing the whole created order, redeeming and restoring it. As you look back at how you have used nature in prayer, notice how the material is the vehicle of the spiritual, never being the thing that is worshipped, but time and time again drawing us closer to the Lord of all things. Perhaps your prayers and activities have sparked a desire to take action. It could be as simple as growing some leaves in a window box. It might involve some kind of community action to care for the environment or supporting a charity that seeks to help people find healing through involvement with the natural world. Using nature to draw close to God will lead us to a more robust and mature faith if we open ourselves to God our creator and redeemer, who cares about human beings so much that he came to earth and lived among us (John 1:14).

Praying with objects

Lisa Cherrett

Gathering objects

Introduction

Picture this! When Jesus wanted to explain aspects of the kingdom of God or of faith to his first followers out on the hills and lake shores of Galilee, he often spoke in picture language. He used images of activities and objects that everyone knew and understood – talking about baking bread, sowing seed, lighting lamps and caring for animals. Nothing was too ordinary or mundane to be used as an aid to understanding, to galvanise people into making a response to him, with their imaginations engaged and their wills inspired to live closer to their Father God.

When we come to a time of prayer, we too can use ordinary everyday objects to help us reflect on God's ways. Over the next two weeks I'd like to encourage you to take three objects – a key or bunch of keys, a map and a mirror – and see if they might help to lead you further into prayer. None of these objects are mentioned very often in the Bible, though we might think of them as indispensable in our lives today. Nevertheless, in the places where they are mentioned or implied, there are some interesting lessons we can learn and pointers to aspects of discipleship that we might wish to deepen.

So, see if you can gather those three objects from around the house. It can be any sort of key, the map should be a road map if possible, and the mirror a portable one that shows your face, such as a compact or bathroom mirror. Place them in front of you and make a start by coming to the Lord in prayer, saying:

Heavenly Father, who gives authority, direction and self-knowledge, help me to draw closer to you over the coming days, to learn from you through these everyday objects, and to put what I learn into practice. In Jesus' name. Amen

Keys and locks

Reflection

Pick up a key of any sort in your hand. It might be a door key, a car key or something much smaller, such as one that unlocks a suitcase, jewellery box or musical instrument. Think back to the day when you were given this key. How did it feel to be entrusted with it for the first time? Take a moment to remember, and perhaps write down a word or two to describe your emotions.

Now fit your key into the lock for which it was designed, or imagine doing so if the relevant lock is not accessible. How does it feel to turn the key, to hear it engage with the internal mechanisms, and to see the door or case spring open, or hear the engine turn over? Write down some words to describe how it feels.

One element in your feelings about keys and unlocking might be 'excitement'. The *Dictionary of Biblical Imagery* says, 'A key (even in ancient times) is a relatively small thing compared to that which it opens' (Leland Ryken et al., eds, IVP Academic, 1998, p. 476), and so to use a key to unlock something is to open up a world of bigger possibilities – comfort and security, or treasure of some sort, or freedom to travel and explore.

I wonder if this helps us to understand one aspect of what Jesus meant when he said to the apostle Peter, 'I will give you the keys of the kingdom of heaven' (Matthew 16:19). For us as believers in Jesus, the kingdom of heaven is a world of possibilities waiting to be unlocked – our true home, a box of treasure, a licence to explore new territories. Does this idea excite you? How might it change the way you approach your Christian journey? Write down a few of your thoughts.

Keys for others

Intercession

In the Christian life, the gifts we are given by God are never meant to be kept for our own use or benefit. They are intended to be used or shared in service to other people as well. So it is with the keys of the kingdom of God. According to the *Dictionary of Biblical Imagery*, again, 'keys are images of trust and responsibility' (p. 476). The keyholder has a responsibility to use them wisely on behalf of the one who has entrusted them to him or her.

Jesus often felt the need to rebuke and correct the religious leaders of his day, and on one occasion he said to the teachers of the law, 'Woe to you… because you have taken away the key to knowledge. You yourselves have not entered, and you have hindered those who were entering' (Luke 11:52). So, if we have been entrusted with keys to the kingdom of God, we need to be careful not to 'take them away' from others but to help others to enter the kingdom with us.

Look back at the words you wrote down to describe how it feels when you turn a key to unlock something. Can you think of anyone – a friend, family member, neighbour or workmate – who needs to feel those emotions? Is there someone who is locked into a bad situation, who needs release from it? Write down their name or names in your prayer journal or on a piece of card, and draw a key next to the name(s). In prayer, ask God to turn the key that will release them into new possibilities.

Perhaps they have tried different 'keys' already to solve their problem or open the way forward, but nothing has worked. Ask God to find exactly the right key to fit into their locked situation. Remember that God himself holds the key to each person's heart, uniquely fitted because of his uniquely intimate knowledge of each one of us.

Lost keys

Reflection

What exactly are the 'keys' that unlock the kingdom of heaven? What keys have you discovered during your Christian journey that have helped you unlock the kingdom of heaven?

Take a sheet of paper and write or draw as many ideas as you can think of.

Here are some suggestions to start your thinking:

- Knowledge of God's word in the Bible
- Persistent, trusting prayer
- Faith in Jesus, rather than in our own righteousness (Galatians 3:22–25)
- Childlike trust and simplicity
- The proclamation of the gospel (Luke 4:43)
- Speaking the truth (John 8:32)
- Praise and thankfulness

Do you have a whole bunch of kingdom keys to use? Which do you use most often and which have been neglected – gone rusty from lack of use?

In our world, there is a great fear associated with keys – the fear that they might be lost or, worse, stolen. Keys are given to trusted and authorised people, but what happens when untrustworthy or unauthorised people get hold of them? The same fear attaches, in today's technology-focused society, to the passwords that we use for access to important internet sites, email or social media accounts.

Look again at your list of keys. Do you feel as if any of them have been lost or stolen from you? Don't be afraid! Remember that, ultimately, Jesus himself is the holder of the keys. They belong to him, and he can find them and give them back to us. If you fear that you have lost some keys that you used to have, ask him to entrust you with them once again. You may want to add a key to your keyring as a regular reminder of the 'keys' God has given you.

Finding our way home

Reflection

Today, put aside your keys and look at your map – preferably a road atlas.

It is perhaps unlikely that maps were used in biblical times, although navigation by the stars would have been known, especially by sailors. However, the biblical writers were aware of the importance of finding a safe, secure way to a destination. Psalm 107 talks about the distress of those who 'wandered in desert wastelands, finding no way to a city where they could settle' (v. 4) and others who 'went out on the sea in ships' only to encounter 'a tempest that lifted high the waves' (vv. 23, 25). In both cases, their desperate cries to the Lord resulted in guidance from him: 'He led them by a straight way to a city where they could settle… he guided them to their desired haven' (vv. 7, 30).

Where is your physical place of settlement, your 'desired haven'? Can you find it on your road map? Perhaps it's the town where you live at present, or your childhood home, or a place where you dream of living one day. Or perhaps you have no particular place that you would call 'home' at the moment and can only keep turning the pages of the map without finding a place on which to 'settle'.

How do you feel about this? Secure and happy, blessed in the place where you find yourself? If so, thank God that 'the boundary lines have fallen for me in pleasant places' (Psalm 16:6). Or are you restless and distracted, wishing you could be somewhere else? If so, ask God if this is a healthy restlessness – if he is guiding you to consider a move for good reasons – or if you are resisting his call to stay where you are. Place yourself and your loved ones in his hands and ask for his peace to come, in whatever way he sees is best for you. Perhaps, of course, you thrive on adventure and do not especially need a place to settle. If this is your gift, ask God to use it for the furtherance of his kingdom.

Wherever you are on the map, and however you feel about it, remember that 'here we do not have an enduring city, but we are looking for the city that is to come' (Hebrews 13:14; see Revelation 21:2–4). Thank God for the hope that this offers us all for the future.

A straight way

Reflection

'He led them by a straight way to a city where they could settle' (Psalm 107:7). On a road map of Britain, it's interesting to look for the Roman roads – those dead straight highways leading to and from towns that were important Roman settlements, such as Cirencester in Gloucestershire, or the city of Lincoln. I describe them as 'highways' but, in fact, many of them have by now been relegated to B road status. You may have to look for the narrow yellow roads lurking apologetically beside the more important red A roads, green trunk roads and blue motorways. Some Roman roads are just rough pathways, unmarked on the map. I think of one, near my home, which is clearly visible as two straight muddy tracks across a field, stretching off into the distance as the main road diverges from it. It's no longer considered a feasible route for our cars and buses.

Open your road atlas and see if you can spot any Roman roads. (One example might be the A429, becoming the B4455, which runs north-east from Moreton-in-Marsh in Gloucestershire, passing to the east of Stratford-upon-Avon and Leamington Spa.)

In the Bible, a straight road is always a good road: 'Trust in the Lord with all your heart… in all your ways submit to him, and he will make your paths straight' (Proverbs 3:5–6); 'Lead me, Lord, in your righteousness because of my enemies – make your way straight before me' (Psalm 5:8). A straight road is the most direct route. A straight road is an honest road, allowing you to see a long way ahead and to spot obstacles before they trip you up.

Is your path in life straight at the moment – open and honest and without obstacles, so that you can stride out freely and without too much anxiety along it? Or are there traps and tricky bends to manoeuvre around? How might God make your paths straighter for you? Bear in mind that the straight path might be the B road – a way that seems less obvious, less well travelled, but is actually the safest and most direct route to take.

Path of life

Creative

Take a large sheet of paper and some coloured pencils or pens in blue, red, green and yellow, and an ordinary lead pencil. Can you draw a road map of your life so far, or a portion of it – perhaps the last year or two? How would you picture it in terms of the types of road you will see on a printed map? The busiest, most hectic times might be shown as motorways, in blue. The quietest or most solitary times might be in yellow for rural B roads, whether straight or twisting. The in-between times of steady progress could be shown as green or red A roads.

If you've experienced paths in life that seem to have taken you to dead ends, or events that have made no sense, you could show them in pencil, as if they were the farm tracks or other very minor roads that are not graced with names or numbers. Add landmarks or monuments to your route. Use your imagination to depict important events in some way.

As you look at the road map of your life, spend some time in silence, simply offering it up to God in prayer. What does he say to you about it?

Our future route is unknown to us. Even if we think the way ahead is already mapped out for us, there can be unexpected twists and turns in the road. At the end of the map you have drawn, where it becomes the unknown future, draw a fork in the road and write next to it a verse from the Bible that assures you of God's presence and guidance – for example, 'Whether you turn to the right or to the left, your ears will hear a voice behind you, saying, "This is the way; walk in it"' (Isaiah 30:21).

Look in the mirror

Reflection

The final object that I shall suggest as an aid to prayer may be an unpopular, even very challenging, choice, but I hope you will be able to stay with it. Pick up a mirror in which you can see your face – a hand mirror, a compact mirror or a bathroom mirror – or, if you would prefer, stand in front of a full-length mirror. What is your immediate reaction – 'Yes, not bad' or 'Please take it away'?

Whatever your feelings when you see yourself, offer those emotions to God in prayer for a few moments. Then turn the mirror away from you or stand away so that you can no longer see your reflection. Close your eyes and meditate for a while on God's words to Samuel when he went to Jesse's house to choose a new king of Israel: 'The Lord does not look at the things people look at. People look at the outward appearance, but the Lord looks at the heart' (1 Samuel 16:7).

Is it more challenging, or less, to know that when God looks at you, he sees your heart, not your physical appearance? Remind yourself that he looks with love, not harsh judgement, with a view to perfecting us, not condemning (Romans 8:1).

End your time of meditation with a prayer from Psalm 139: 'Search me, God, and know my heart; test me and know my anxious thoughts. See if there is any offensive way in me, and lead me in the way everlasting' (vv. 23–24).

The word of God as a mirror

Bible study/creative

Read James 1:22–25. This is one of the very few places where a mirror is mentioned in the Bible, and it is used as an illustration of how pointless it is to read the word of God without allowing it to change us in some way. If we look in a mirror and notice that a crucial button is undone or that we're about to leave the house still wearing our slippers, we immediately put the problem right. In the same way, James suggests that our reading of the Bible might give us hints of things in our hearts that need correcting.

How does the Bible do this? It might be by presenting us with lists of bad qualities and actions, contrasted with good ones, as in Galatians 5:19–23. Or it might be by showing us the mixed weaknesses and strengths of God's followers in the Old and New Testaments, such as King David or the apostle Peter, as examples of discipleship. If we study these Bible stories and passages (and note that James says we should 'look intently', not just give a cursory glance), we may see ourselves reflected to some extent, and be able to pinpoint areas of our own lives that we would like to see changed.

Is there a Bible character with whom you identify, because you share their strengths or failings, or one whom you admire as someone whose faith inspires you? Draw an outline figure of this character, with his or her name at the centre, and jot down some of those characteristics, both good and bad, around the outside.

Spend some time praying about your own attitudes and actions, compared to this person from the Bible. How can you make the changes that you think God would like to see in you?

Alternatively, if there is something in a biblical list of qualities, either good or bad, that strikes you as especially relevant in your life, pray about how it might inspire you to change.

Reflecting the light

Reflection

Another well-known passage in the Bible that talks about a mirror is 1 Corinthians 13:12: 'For now we see only a reflection as in a mirror; then we shall see face to face. Now I know in part; then I shall know fully, even as I am fully known.' God sees and knows us fully and intimately (Psalm 139), but we cannot possibly look on him face to face. We would be blinded by the intensity of his light. Nonetheless, the more we get to know God, incomplete as our knowledge must be, the more we are transformed into his image and the more we should reflect his image to the people around us (2 Corinthians 3:18).

Hold up your portable mirror and, instead of looking into it, turn it away from yourself. Find a source of light – either sunlight through the window or an electric lamp – and see if you can catch it in the mirror, bouncing it around the walls of your room. With a mirror, a little light can go a long way.

You might think, too, of the way the moon acts as a mirror to the sun. It's dangerous to look directly at the sun: its light is too bright for our delicate eyes, just as God's holiness is too bright for us. But the moon, with no light of its own, reflects the rays of the sun with an intensity that is both bearable and beautiful. A full moon in a cloudless sky can shed a surprising amount of light on our path, dispelling the darkness of night. Perhaps we can reflect God's glory in a dark world, in the same way.

As you come to God in prayer, ask that you might become, more and more as time goes by, a mirror to his light, bouncing it around the places in which you find yourself.

Mirror image in paint

Creative

Find an A4 or larger sheet of paper. Fold it in half and then open it out again. On one side, using very wet paint or ink, draw an oval outline to represent a mirror. Then, inside the oval, quickly paint something to represent a characteristic of God that you would like to reflect to the world, such as his glory or his love. You might paint the sun with rays spreading out from the centre, a blazing fire or a large heart. Use whatever colours you think are appropriate.

Then, before the paint or ink dries, fold your paper in half again to make a mirror image of your painting on the other side.

You might like to add some words from 2 Corinthians 3:18: 'We all, with unveiled faces, reflect the Lord's glory.'

Hang up your picture as a reminder to pray for transformation each day.

Keys, maps and mirrors

Liturgy

You might like to sum up your experience of praying with keys, maps and mirrors in the words of this prayer.

> *Lord Jesus, you hold the keys of the kingdom of God. Thank you for the wonderful possibilities that these keys open up. Thank you that you entrust them to me. Help me to keep them safe and to use them wisely, for the benefit of others as well as myself. Where there are problems in my life or the lives of people I know, help me to find the key and unlock your solution, bringing all the blessings of your kingdom.*

Heavenly Father, you guide us along the paths of our life. Thank you that although we might never be totally at rest in this world, you give us some places to call 'home'. Thank you that as we travel, you show us the 'straight' roads. Help us, whenever we face a choice in life – a fork, or a crossroads – to listen for your voice behind us telling us the way, and help us to follow it, trusting in you.

All-seeing God, you see and know us clearly and without distortion. Thank you that you show us our faults and weaknesses, not to condemn us but to help us change, so that we in turn might see you a little more clearly. Help us to have courage to look intently into your word, and help us not to forget what it shows us about ourselves, but to take whatever action is required. Help us, day by day, to reflect your goodness more brightly to the dark world around us. Amen

Imagining prayer

Sally Smith

Using the imagination

Introduction

For some people, using the imagination as they pray is as natural as breathing. They hear a story and see the pictures immediately in their mind. They notice automatically where Jesus is and are happy to talk to him and hear his response as they pray. For others, it is a different story; they feel they can't begin to imagine a scene and instead find themselves getting wrapped up in whether it's real and how accurate the description is.

The events of the final week of Jesus' life are ideal for entering into imaginatively. It gives the opportunity to be part of the action and to spend time with Jesus during that crucial period. If you find this hard, you're not alone. Try taking the snippets you receive and leaving behind the images that get in the way. You may find you can't see details, so go with the general impressions. You may struggle to see it as an action video, so go with a series of still photos, entering each in turn and noticing what you experience there. Many people struggle to see Jesus' face. If this happens use an outline, or the sense of a person instead. Use what God gives rather than fighting for what is not there.

Be prepared to spend time setting the scene, to notice what is around you, using all your senses to create the full picture. If this is particularly hard you might want to search for some pictures online or in books that will help set the scene. Take just one image so you aren't distracted by too many choices or too much detail.

For some people it helps to be outside enacting the scene – walking with Jesus as he carries his cross or with the disciples on their way to Emmaus, or by the sea as he calls his disciples to follow him. You are not aiming at a historically accurate re-creation of a scene, you are aiming at an encounter with God, and so give him room within your time to make himself known, and give yourself room to notice him.

Begin by choosing a chair in your room. Imagine Jesus sitting on that chair. Where do you want to be – near him or by the door, standing, sitting on another chair, kneeling at his feet or resting your head on his lap? Move to where you feel comfortable. Don't judge yourself for where you are; Jesus will not do so. Allow the scene to unfold. You may watch him, or talk to him, or shout at him, or just be with him. He may beckon you, or talk to you or just enjoy your company. Allow Jesus and yourself to say and do all you need, and allow time to be in each other's company.

When you are ready, return to where you were before you started and acknowledge where you have been. If you have not been able to imagine this, tell Jesus about it in your usual way – expressing your desire and what you want from him.

Some of the passages in this section will fit well into Holy Week and some will be appropriate at any time, so you may want to pick those that suit the day as we approach Easter.

Burning bush

Imaginative

Read Exodus 3:1–6.

Though we are focusing on the New Testament as we approach Easter, the Old Testament contains a wealth of stories we can use to meet with God. When an angel appears to Moses in a burning bush in the desert, he has an encounter with God such that he recognises the land as holy. It leads to a long conversation with God and, as with many such encounters, he is afraid to look at God. So as you approach God in your imagination, notice also what is happening inside you: how you are feeling and how you respond.

Begin by setting the scene. Moses is in the wilderness with his father-in-law's flock of sheep. See the bareness and the open spaces. Feel the heat and the wind, feel the sand and rocks beneath your feet. Listen to the stillness of the desert and the noise of the flock. Relax into the slow, quiet way of life. Watch Moses as he moves among his sheep.

You see a bush that appears to be burning but is not being consumed. There is an angel in the fire. Notice where you are and how you react. Then notice what Moses is doing.

Listen as God speaks to Moses (read the words from Exodus 3:5–6). You may imagine drawing closer to the bush, or removing your shoes as you kneel or stand before God.

Spend time with God on this holy ground before the burning bush.

When you are ready, leave the imagined scene behind and return to the room where you are and to the present time. Re-run what has just occurred in your mind and notice where God has been and what he has said. Notice the surprises you have had.

Go to a high place

Intercession/going out

As well as using our imagination to encounter God, we can use it to intercede for others.

Imagine standing in a high place above a city or town you know well. If you are struggling, you might prefer to go to that place and do this exercise there.

Imagine looking out at the scene. Pick out the places you know well and the places you don't know so well.

Then imagine God standing next to you joining you in seeing the city. How does this change your attitude to what you see? How does the focus of your viewing change?

You may begin to talk to him about what you see, but then pause and listen. How does God see the scene before you? Where is his focus and how does he feel about what he sees?

Ask what he wants you to do about what you see and where you can best serve him in this place.

When you are both ready, leave the high place and return to your room. Re-play the conversation and note anything that has been significant for you.

Feeding of the 5,000

Imaginative

Read Matthew 14:13–21.

Using your imagination in prayer is especially effective with Bible passages with plenty of action and where something significant and visual happens. This is particularly the case with the miracles Jesus performed, both the healing miracles and others such as the feeding of the 5,000.

Imagine you are one of Jesus' disciples, sitting close by him outside on a hillside. Picture the scene. There is a crowd with thousands of people. You have been there several hours. Look around you at the people who are there, whole families, children and older people, men and women. They are enjoying listening to Jesus talk and watching him heal people. How do you feel after this long day with Jesus and the crowds? Look at the crowds of people; watch them for a while, the children playing and the adults listening. Some who are ill are trying to get close to Jesus, asking for healing.

Enjoy the scene, noticing some individuals and maybe joining in some of their conversations.

But eventually you notice the sun is getting lower and the people have a restlessness about them. You realise it must be getting late and that you are getting hungry. With a few of the other disciples you approach Jesus: 'This is a deserted place, and the hour is now late; send the crowds away so that they may go into the villages and buy food for themselves.'

Jesus looks at you and replies, 'They need not go away; you give them something to eat.'

Think about this for a moment and notice what your internal response is before replying, 'We have nothing here but five loaves and two fish.'

Jesus asks you to bring the fish and loaves to him. As you fetch them you hear Jesus ordering the crowd to sit down on the grass.

You watch as he takes the bread and the fish, looks to heaven, blesses and breaks the loaves.

He gives you and the other disciples some of the bread and fish to pass to the crowd. You start breaking it and giving it out to the people gathered.

When all are fed, you join the other disciples and sit and eat the bread and fish. Enjoy the food and the meal eaten together.

When you are finished you find some baskets and begin collecting the leftover food from the crowd. Chat to the people as you gather and watch the basket filling.

You hand your basket back to Jesus and he looks at you and says your name. What do you reply? Spend as long as you need with Jesus before he sends you on your way and stays to dismiss the crowd.

Back in your room, recall the events and how you felt and responded to different stages of the action. Where did you feel the presence of Jesus most clearly? What did Jesus say to you, and what did you say to him?

You might like to make some notes in your journal if you keep one.

Pool at Beth-zatha

Imaginative

One of the concerns given about using the imagination in prayer is that it becomes an imaginative exercise and is not real. Before you pray, invite the Holy Spirit to enter your imagination and to inspire your thoughts. Ask God to work through your imagination and to be present as you pray. After your prayer session spend time with God, offering what you have received so that he may filter out your imagination and emphasise his message.

Many of the accounts of Jesus are suitable for using in this way. In the healing at Beth-zatha (also written as Bethesda) we read of an encounter between an ill man and Jesus and how the man is healed. In this you can imagine being with Jesus, or being the man who is healed. As always, adapt the instructions below to fit your situation.

Read John 5:2–9.

Now imagine the scene. See the pool and the five porticoes.

See the many sick – blind, disabled and paralysed.

Listen to the noise and the chatter.

Then Jesus arrives and goes to one man in particular. Follow Jesus as he greets the man and asks if he wants to be made well.

Listen to the reply, 'Sir, I have no one to put me into the pool when the water is stirred up; and while I am making my way, someone else steps down ahead of me.'

Listen as Jesus says to him, 'Stand up, take your mat and walk.'

Watch as the man gets up for the first time in 38 years and begins to walk. Notice his reaction and that of those around him.

When the man has gone, Jesus turns to you and asks, 'What do you want from me?' How do you answer? What is your first 'gut' reaction? Go with this one – he knows it already and it may surprise you. Spend as long as you need with Jesus before returning from your imagination to the room where you are sitting.

Anointing at Bethany

Imaginative

Read Matthew 26:6–13.

As Jesus prepares for that final journey to Jerusalem, he is anointed with oil. We join the disciples at Bethany, at the home of Simon the leper.

Imagine the disciples sitting around the low table. They have been eating a meal and the remains are left for us to see. Notice where you are in the room – are you seated by Jesus, or do you place yourself at a distance? You might imagine you are one of the disciples, or the woman who is about to appear. Take the role that seems to draw you most. Don't worry about accuracy or getting it 'right'; this is about how you encounter Jesus now and how he uses your imagination to do that.

So look about the room. Listen to the conversations going on; you might join in one of them.

Then a woman walks into the room and quietly approaches Jesus. She takes a small alabaster jar and opens it. Smell the ointment as she pours it over his head. How does Jesus react? How do you react?

You feel and hear the anger of the disciples, 'Why this waste? For this ointment could have been sold for a large sum, and the money given to the poor.' Do you join in the anger?

Hear Jesus respond, 'Why do you trouble the woman? She has performed a good service for me. For you always have the poor with you, but you will not always have me. By pouring this ointment on my body she has prepared me for burial. Truly I tell you, wherever this good news is proclaimed in the whole world, what she has done will be told in remembrance of her.'

Watch as she leaves the room and the disciples settle again. Then Jesus turns to you. What do you say to him?

Allow time for him to speak to you, letting the conversation play out in your imagination, before returning to the room where you are sitting.

The last supper

Imaginative

Read Matthew 26:26–30.

The disciples move to another house and another room. Join them as one of the disciples as they celebrate the Passover meal. Imagine the food spread before you. The disciples are reclining around a low table. Listen to their conversations; they may be talking about some of the things Jesus has been saying to them recently and trying to decide what he means by some of the phrases he keeps using.

Jesus takes the bread from the table and lifts it up to bless it. He breaks it and gives a chunk to each disciple, including you. He says to you, 'Take, eat; this is my body.'

Watch as the others receive the bread from Jesus.

He then takes a cup of wine, raises it and gives thanks for it. He passes it to the nearest disciple and says, 'Drink from it, all of you, for this is my blood of the covenant, which is poured out for many for the forgiveness of sins. I tell you, I will never again drink of this fruit of the vine until that day when I drink it new with you in my Father's kingdom.'

When the cup is passed to you, drink from the cup. What does this mean to you in this moment?

The meal continues and Jesus turns to you. What do you say to him, and how does he respond to you? Stay in this conversation for as long as you need before returning to the room where you are sitting.

It can be helpful to write in your journal, if you have one, what has happened, noticing in particular anything that surprised you, and what Jesus said in your conversations. This helps clarify what did happen, makes what Jesus said clearer and helps you recognise the significance of your prayer.

The garden at Gethsemane

Imaginative/going out

Read Matthew 26:36–46.

Sometimes it can help the imagination to be in a place similar to that you are imagining. You might want to go outside into your garden, or to a favourite outdoor place where you will be alone.

Imagine the scene of the garden of Gethsemane. Picture a garden; you may use a garden you know, or imagine a garden with olive trees and rough ground. Notice the stars above. Listen to the people passing by and the wind in the trees. Spend some time in the garden, noticing the sights and sounds, enjoying the peace of the evening.

Then you begin to notice the people in the garden with you. You are with a group of men. Listen in to their conversation. Watch how they group and re-group.

Jesus and three others leave the rest and go to a quieter place. Do you follow, or watch from a distance? Jesus says to Peter and the two sons of Zebedee, 'I am deeply grieved, even to death; remain here, and stay awake with me.' He goes off further and throws himself on the ground to pray.

You hear him say, 'My Father, if it is possible, let this cup pass from me; yet not what I want but what you want.'

Try to stay awake and watch with Jesus and his disciples. Three times Jesus comes back to you and finds the disciples sleeping. He commands them to stay awake and pray 'that you may not come into the time of trial; the spirit indeed is willing, but the flesh is weak'.

As he returns for the third time, what do you say and what does Jesus say to you? Notice how you feel as you meet him after your watching time.

Peter denies Jesus

Imaginative

Read Matthew 26:69–75 and then imagine being in a courtyard in Jerusalem. Notice who is there, gathered around in small groups: there are slaves and soldiers standing there, guarding Jesus. Listen to their conversations.

Feel the cold and be drawn towards a burner in the courtyard. Notice how you try to hide as you get some warmth from the fire.

A girl approaches you saying, 'You also were with Jesus the Galilean.' Without thinking you deny you were there or any knowledge of what she's talking about.

Feel her staring at you and move away. Another servant-girl says to her friends, 'This man was with Jesus of Nazareth.' To which you reply, 'I do not know the man.'

As you wait, a bystander comes and says, 'Certainly you are also one of them, for your accent betrays you.' You curse and swear, 'I do not know the man!' and you hear the sound of a cock crowing.

Respond as you need to.

On the cross

Imaginative

On Good Friday, try to spend some time at the foot of the cross. This might be a physical cross in a church or somewhere nearby, or a small one at home, or you might imagine being with Jesus' disciples and the women as they gather around Jesus for his last few hours on earth. Read Matthew 27:32–56.

Return to the streets of Jerusalem. Imagine the crowds pressing into the narrow passages. Feel the stone beneath your feet. Hear the noises of the people, the calling and shouting and the muttered conversations. Smell the sweaty bodies around you and the food being cooked in the adjoining houses. Become part of the mass of people in this busy place. It might help to remember how you felt in a similar crowd in the past.

You hear shouts of soldiers, calling to clear the way. They push through, followed by Jesus hauling a huge cross. Watch as he struggles to move, to carry the great weight, to put one foot in front of the other in this chaotic street, as he focuses totally on the task he is involved with. Watch his mother and others follow him, and maybe join in their wailing.

Allow the events to unfold, as Simon of Cyrene is ordered to carry the cross, as the crowds shout and jeer and the procession leaves the city walls, heading for the bleak Place of the Skull.

See the other two crosses and hear the hammering of the nails and the continuing wailing of the women following Jesus.

And then, wait in the darkness.

Where do you go to wait – close to the cross, by the others, or on the edge with strangers? What is happening for you in the waiting?

Don't rush – this is a time for waiting and for being by the cross. You may draw near to Jesus; what do you say or do? You may join his remaining followers; who do you relate to?

And then, wait.

Jesus cries out, 'Eli, Eli, lema sabachthani!' Bystanders mutter and Jesus breathes his last.

The earth shakes and rocks are split and the guards cry, 'Truly this man was God's Son!'

And you quietly walk away.

Easter day

Imaginative

Read Luke 24:1–12.

The time for rejoicing in public comes at the great celebrations on Easter morning in church. Before that comes the quiet realisation and meeting with the risen Christ that occurred in the garden on the first Easter morning.

So, you are invited to join Mary Magdalene and Mary the mother of James and Salome as they set off to anoint the body of Jesus which has been left in the tomb over the Sabbath.

Imagine that walk together in the early morning, each with your own memories of Jesus and the events of the previous few years, and of the past week. Which events do you recall in particular; maybe some you have explored this week, or other favourite encounters with Jesus.

As you approach the tomb you wonder who you will be able to get to roll the stone away and open the tomb for you. But you reach the tomb and the stone has moved.

How does it feel as you enter the tomb? You find it is empty.

Suddenly there are two men in bright, dazzling clothes standing in front of you.

What do you feel and what do you do?

'Why do you look for the living among the dead? He is not here, but has risen. Remember how he told you, while you were still in Galilee, that the Son of Man must be handed over to sinners, and be crucified, and on the third day rise again.'

Remember those words; allow them time to sink in and the reality of what they mean to become apparent to you.

The women turn and run back to tell the other followers what they have seen. You remain by the tomb and let Jesus find you there. Rest by the tomb with the risen Christ. You may find you stay there for a long time, until Peter comes, or it may be time for you to leave quietly before they arrive.

Keep imagining

Imaginative

We have journeyed through the Holy Week and Easter story in our imaginations. Hopefully you have encountered Christ as you have journeyed. We have also tried some Old Testament passages and using the imagination without a biblical passage.

Take some time to reflect on which you have found easiest and which have brought you closest to God. What have been the surprises for you, and what have been the struggles?

You may want to try with other Bible passages. Read the passage first, and then put your Bible down. Pray and ask God to inspire your imagination and to remind you of the details you need. Spend time setting the scene, imagining yourself there, using all your senses to get a realistic picture of where the action will take place. You can imagine being one of the main characters, or you can be on the sidelines, watching. Notice where or who you are, but don't analyse it.

When you have finished you may ask why you were that person or why you positioned yourself there, but as the action unfolds, enter into the events and experience all that is happening at the time. Don't be in a rush to get on to the climax of the story, but allow it to go at its own pace; often the waiting and sitting can be as powerful as the miraculous.

End by spending time with God, listening and talking, or enjoying being in his presence, and then replay the time in your imagination, noticing your responses and your thoughts as you do so.

Time of resurrection

Janet Lunt

Introduction

Bible reading

Amid egg hunts and spring flowers, miniature Easter gardens and stirring hymns, we ponder again the resurrection of Jesus and its essential place in the story of reconciliation between God and humanity. In our quiet spaces, we will reflect afresh on its meaning in our own story.

The effect Christianity has had in shaping the world is truly remarkable. Encounters with Jesus were shared by word of mouth only, until written down a few decades later. Up to the point of the tomb in the Gospel stories, Christ's actions and words come across as confident history, but coverage of his resurrection appearances is sketchy and sometimes confusing as details don't always tally across the Gospels. Yet the accounts feel encouragingly authentic because no writers bent on winning the world through words would have presented such raw reactions of disbelief and shock, nor at that time would they have chosen to reveal that women were first on the scene. The overall effect is like peering into a kaleidoscope: we see light through coloured fragments and sense something vibrant and exciting, yet are left to piece together our own picture, like pondering a parable. The brief, unexpected encounters with the risen Jesus seem personal, as if tailor-made to draw out faith according to the character of each follower; this would make sense of their fleeting nature. Above all, these texts allow space for us today to meet the risen Christ in a unique and personal way.

Imagine you are living at that time, and four friends have written to tell you what they have heard or experienced of the events. Read through the resurrection accounts (Matthew 28; Mark 16; Luke 24; John 20, 21), noticing their differing emphases as you allow an overall picture to form.

How do you respond after reading these letters?

An unexpected Easter

Story/creative

One memorable and unusual Easter day, I got up in the dark to attend a sunrise service out in a field. The dawn came masked in greyness and drizzle. Spirits dampened, we stood around under umbrellas, our hopes of watching the sun rising as a symbol of Christ's resurrection dashed. However, towards the end of the service, the hidden sun began to penetrate the mizzle and a rainbow formed, arching above the table of bread and wine like an apse. Its presence affected us all. Later, I realised how fitting the quiet appearance of the rainbow had been, for the resurrection of Jesus was not accompanied by heavenly choirs or trumpets and no one witnessed his rising. Like a rainbow, his appearances were brief, unexpected and compelling.

We cannot look directly at sunlight, but we can look at the glowing colours it is made up of when refracted through raindrops. We cannot look at the Lord directly or experience resurrection yet, but we can encounter him in many ways.

Sit with the tomb on that first Easter eve for a while and allow the resurrection of Jesus to slowly become known to you. It may come as quietly as the rainbow or the rising sun – use whatever imagery helps you. If you have found celebration difficult this

Easter, it may be especially helpful to use the gentle images in the quiet before facing the rejoicing of the discovery and the spreading of the news.

Call to mind 'rainbow moments' in your life: perhaps a time when struggle has been resolved, when a timely scripture has blessed you, or when prayer has quietly come to fruition. Give thanks to God for these significant little Easters. Find a rainbow image to use as a desktop background, or create a rainbow bookmark with card and colours or a photograph.

The hidden place

Imaginative

Read John 20:19–22.

After the crucifixion, the disciples hid away in a locked room, broken and afraid. The ability of the risen Lord to come to the rescue of trembling, fearful people, even within a locked room, is a great encouragement of how Jesus can enter into the secret place of our hearts.

Light a candle, and observe the extraordinary nature of the flame; gently breathe on it and watch its movement. Ready yourself for meditation by sitting comfortably but alert. Take in a few deep breaths, exhaling slowly: as you do this, be conscious of life-giving air entering your body which then departs in the altered state of carbon dioxide, while oxygen sustains you. Allow stillness to descend...

You are in a locked room, waiting...

Recent events have been disturbing, and you sense nothing will be the same again... the future feels uncertain, fragile. You register how your heart feels right now, noticing any restriction, emptiness, fear, disturbance...

You cannot find meaningful words to pray, so you wait in silence, with deep longing; your longing is your prayer…

Instances come to mind when you have felt near to Jesus, and you call to mind an occasion when hope and eternity were almost tangible… You envisage him at work… healing people of sickness… speaking to crowds…

Suddenly, the room is transformed with light and warmth… it is the Lord! You absorb the warm light, and notice how your heart reacts… The Lord greets you by name, and you respond… he draws close to you, so close you can hear his breathing… you speak with him, asking any questions, telling him of anything that troubles your heart…

Jesus says to you: 'Peace be with you!' You allow his special peace to take effect… and note how it feels. 'Receive the Holy Spirit', he says as he breathes over you… you breathe in his gift, the Breath of Life itself…

You express your thankfulness… and listen to anything he might say to you, any instructions he might give… In the Lord's presence you rest for as long as you choose.

When you are ready, blow out the candle.

Empty space

Reflective

When someone close to us dies, we are advised to attend the funeral, even to view their body, so we face the reality and begin the process of closure. In a strangely similar way, it appeared it was important for the disciples of Jesus to experience the empty tomb – all four Gospels mention it. Both Marys, who witnessed the burial of Jesus, expected his lifeless body to be there, because they carried spices to anoint him. In Luke's account, they and the others who investigated were shocked by the empty void – it was pregnant with meaning but, as yet, not understood. We know the story so well that it's hard to imagine their reaction. But remembering they were in deep grief, it makes sense that they needed time to process what Christ's resurrection meant, its implications for them and for their faith. The empty tomb was the introduction, important for the disciples and Jerusalem society alike.

Unexpected voids that appear in our own lives can be difficult to handle. We might lose someone we love deeply, or a significant role. We may have to face a long spell of waiting, spiritual emptiness or loss of fellowship. How do we react to sudden space? Maybe we try to fill it as quickly as possible. How do we face a void that plunges us into shock, fear, grief or darkness? In an Easter poem, Kathy Galloway writes, 'Now there is nowhere we can go, no darkness we can enter, which is not God-encompassed' (*Looking in the Wrong Places*, Wild Goose Publications). She reminds us that Jesus entered the darkest places any of us have to face, and lived again.

The void of the empty tomb was a prelude to extraordinary encounters. Although Jesus' resurrection may not always mean jumping for joy but sometimes a slowly realised recovery or revelation, we can say, with Julian of Norwich, that all things will be well.

In his sonnet *On the Edge* (from *Sounding the Seasons*, Canterbury Press), Malcolm Guite says, 'The tomb becomes a womb'. Allow this to speak to you. Turn your response into prayer.

Breath of God

Prayer/creative

> Shasta discovered that someone or somebody was walking beside him. It was pitch dark and he could see nothing… What he could hear was breathing… At last, he could bear it no longer. 'Who are you?' he said, scarcely above a whisper… 'Myself,' said the Voice, very deep and low so that the earth shook: and again 'Myself,' loud and clear and gay: and then the third time 'Myself,' whispered so softly you could hardly hear it, and yet it seemed to come from all round you as if the leaves rustled with it. Shasta was no longer afraid that the Voice belonged to something that would eat him, nor that it was the voice of a ghost. But a new and different sort of trembling came over him. Yet he felt glad too.
>
> From *The Horse and His Boy* (ch. 11), 'The Chronicles of Narnia' by C.S. Lewis

The pronunciation of God's name YHWH (the Tetragrammaton), the holiest name in Judaism and often written as Yahweh or Jehovah, is endlessly disputed. One pronunciation among Hebrew-speaking people sounds like Yehuah. In Hebrew-Aramaic the 'h' is pronounced with the breath, representing the Breath of Life. An American rabbi, Arthur Waskow, tells us that YHWH is beyond pronunciation unless breathing counts. He says: 'The notion of YHWH as "the Breath of Life" accords with a deep sense of God as intimate and transcendent at once… Moreover, it makes profound sense for at least one of the real Names of the real God to be not… in any single language, but… in some form of expression that both underlies and transcends language: just breathing' (theshalomcenter.org). The name of Jesus, in Hebrew pronounced Yeshua and meaning 'Yahweh is salvation', carries the breath of the creator's name within it, as does the name of the Holy Spirit (Ruach Hakodesh – *ruach* can also be translated as wind or breath). Perhaps the breathing of the Holy Spirit upon the disciples came through speaking the holy name of the divine Spirit or Breath of God.

Use one of the holy names above by breathing it (whispering) as a way of praying with God's name upon your lips. As you breathe out, gently say YHWH – the pronunciation is unimportant here, God knows you are calling him. Try moving your lips as little as possible and allow your breath to say God's name, and for his breath to join with yours as you breathe.

Looking for signs

Going out/creative

As we age, we can lose our child-like wonder of caterpillars turning into butterflies or tadpoles into frogs yet, nonetheless, each transformation remains extraordinary. Optimistic nature is shot through with resurrection, most evident in springtime. Consider the miracle of how the delicate neck of the snowdrop survives pushing through hardened winter earth, how our bodies can repair themselves after damage and how vegetation springs up among grey ashes in the aftermath of a volcanic eruption. Amazing transformations are going on around and in us. What does this say about the nature of our creator?

God's love is also transforming our inner nature: it is the stuff of resurrection. Each time we recognise our wrong-doings and seek forgiveness from God, or when we forgive others, a miracle takes place. Bring to mind the miracles of transformation that have taken place in your own life so far, and give thanks.

Go for a walk and see, or observe from your window, what has sprung to life along paths, in gardens and hedgerows, even between paving slabs. Notice the earth's cycles, our planet's miraculous renewal of life. Express your wonder to God in praise.

Find some alfalfa or mustard seeds, mung beans or similar. Sprout them in a jar by rinsing through with water and draining, daily. Over the next few days, watch for the miracle of complete change and transformation from hard-cased shells to soft, edible growth.

Faith and doubt

Reflection

> Faith is the bird that feels the light and sings when the dawn is still dark.
> You can't cross the sea merely by standing and staring at the water.
>
> Rabindranath Tagore

Read the story of Thomas in John 20:24–29.

It's possible to journey in faith for a long time then find ourselves in a place of doubt. Sometimes, it is easier to stand at the foot of the cross than gaze into the empty tomb, for resurrection requires a leap of faith way beyond our comfort zone. Of course, faith isn't faith without the possibility of doubt. Jesus expected faith, although not blind faith. He developed a relationship with his followers, living closely with them for three years, teaching about the kingdom of God and performing miracles. Therefore his expectation was closely linked to trust. Even so, the disciples (notably Thomas) were confounded by the empty tomb until their risen Lord himself appeared to them.

Benedictine nun and writer Joan Chittister believes doubt is our saving grace, 'the sure proof that the soul seeks more than what's there. Doubt is not always a burden. It can save us from arrogance, from superiority and from pride. It can make eagles out of sheep... Doubt and faith are essential to one another. Doubt is what makes faith mature' (from *Aspects of the Heart*, 23rd Publications).

Thankfully, Jesus provided Thomas and the others with the assurance they needed to build their faith in preparation for the time when he would leave them. When we act in faith, it is unlikely to be blind faith, for it grows out of nurture and assurance we gain through scripture, through God's nature and from our journey.

Reflect on Jesus' words: 'Blessed are those who have not seen and yet have believed' (John 20:29), considering your place in his thoughts when he said this.

Listen to a piece of wordless music that inspires faith and hope, for example 'The Lark Ascending' by Vaughan Williams (available on YouTube), as you ponder Tagore's words.

At the shoreline

Imaginative

John 21:1–14 is the inspiration for our meditation. I find a beach scene provides a helpful metaphor as the interface between God and humanity, where land represents the earthed and familiar, and the sea represents God – vastly unknowable, powerful and unpredictable.

Light a candle as a symbol of the presence of the living Lord. Sit attentively, but relaxed, quietening your thoughts. When ready, enter into the following meditation:

I have pushed out from land in my prayer-boat, and am fishing for something to feed and sustain me. I am feeling despondent because I have been searching for a long time but have found nothing. Weariness is overcoming me, and I am ready to give up. I drift in and out of concentration...

Suddenly a distant voice reaches my ears. I look towards the shore where a solitary figure stands calling, and I notice a small beach-fire burning nearby. I strain to listen on the wind… I make out the words: 'Friend, haven't you found anything?' I reply… It sounds as though the voice is calling some instructions… to look deeper?… in another direction?… I cup my hand to my ear, and strain to listen…

I marvel that someone has come to the shoreline and is showing concern for my plight… I decide to make the effort to follow the suggestion, casting my net wider, in another direction… I wait… I watch…

There is a sudden, strong tug… and another… Something is happening, changing… I take note of what I see… hear… feel… my catch is almost too large to handle… After great effort, the fruit is on board and I rejoice with laughter and singing…

I allow the richness and generosity of the vast ocean to overwhelm me with its bounty as I rest in my prayer-boat, complete, sustained… In my heart I know it is the risen Lord who called… I make for the shore as fast as I can to meet him… He invites me to share with him what I have discovered of God's bountiful gift, at the place on the edge between earth and heaven…

Stay in that place on the edge of earth and heaven for as long as you need to.

Christ's lively presence

Intercession

Use the following as a form of intercession. Use the suggestions of areas to pray for or others important to you. Try to visualise Jesus entering the situations you pray for; consider making your prayers visualisations without words. Light a candle.

(To open)

Lord Jesus Christ,
I invite your lively presence through the Holy Spirit
to hear my concerns in prayer.
I ask in faith that you will breathe love and hope into all I pray for:

- for those trapped in poverty by political systems or in the crossfire of war…
- for politicians and decision-makers, for Christ's wisdom to enable justice, peace and freedom…
- for those working for Christian charities, as they seek to be Christ's hands, feet and voice…
- for Christ's love to minister to the suffering, for the terminally ill and their carers…
- for those I love… and those I find hard to love…
- for grace to continue in my own transformation…

(To close)

Risen Christ,
Let the hope of your resurrection and the peace you offer
reach all in need,
through the power of your Holy Spirit.
Amen

The wounds of love

Imaginative

We are given no real explanation as to the nature of Jesus' renewed body. He could appear in a locked room and vanish, yet he said he was not a ghost and proved it by eating. Sometimes, he wasn't recognised immediately and, weeks later, he bodily rose into the clouds. This was unlike the form of raised Lazarus who did not appear or vanish at will and would die again later. One important detail scripture gives us is that Christ's fatal wounds of execution remained on his renewed body. For the disciples, they were physical (forensic) proof, convincing them that Christ had truly returned from death.

Are those scars of Jesus visible in heaven now? Hymn-writer Matthew Bridges believes so: 'Crown him the Lord of love; behold his hands and side, those wounds, yet visible above, in beauty glorified' (1852); it would follow that Jesus ascended with scars still visible. Will they remain for eternity, or be healed when all is made new? Some thinkers believe that Revelation 5:12 indicates they will remain central to worship around the throne forever, as it refers to the 'Lamb who was slain' being worthy to receive honour and praise. Imagine it: human suffering and vulnerability eternally central in the perfection of heaven! Whatever our thoughts about this, it is deeply comforting to have a saviour who is a wounded healer able to identify with our human condition, one who suffered betrayal, desertion, brutality and death before creating future and hope through his rising. His wounds were truly wounds of love.

Sit in a quiet space to pray. (Light a candle if you wish.)

Invite Jesus to sit with you – imagine him being physically present.

Become aware of the scars on his hands/wrists… perhaps you wish to touch them.

Tell Jesus what his wounds mean to you…

Share with him anything you are finding painful – in your own life… in that of another…

Let him reach out with nail-marked hands to comfort, heal and bring hope.

To Emmaus and back

Story (based on Luke 24:13–35)

My dear Naomi,

I write to tell you of the unbelievable things that happened to Cleopas and me, just this week. I guess you heard on the grapevine about the heart-rending death of our beloved teacher, Jesus, accused by some of blasphemy and by others of inciting revolution. Not true! – But I digress. After his crucifixion, we felt there was nothing to stay in Jerusalem for, except the possibility of being arrested as his followers. So we decided to return to Emmaus. As we walked, we tried to work out together how events could possibly have come to this. A stranger, who was going our way, joined us and asked what we were discussing mournfully. Cleopas said he must be the only person not to have heard the headline news in Jerusalem this last week! He didn't react. In fact, he seemed interested, so we told him all about Jesus, explaining he was a prophet from God who spoke powerfully and performed miracles, but our chief priests had accused him of blasphemy, handing him over to the Romans to be crucified. We said we had hoped Jesus would liberate Israel, but now our hope was gone. Then, we described our shock when some women we knew, who also followed Jesus, said they visited the tomb to find it was open and his body gone! And, more shockingly, they had seen angels who said he was alive, sending the men dashing to the garden tomb! But they didn't see Jesus.

When we'd finished our story, this stranger suddenly told us we were fools! He proceeded to expound in detail from our scriptures (Moses and the prophets) how the expected Messiah needed to suffer before entering into his glory, scolding us for not believing the prophecies. Well, we felt ignorant and wished we had faith like him, but also burned with excitement, and longed to hear more. So when we reached Emmaus, we begged him to stay at our place, as it was late. He agreed, so we lit the oil lamps and hurriedly threw supper together.

Now prepare yourself for the biggest shock of all! As we sat down to eat, he picked up the bread, said a blessing, then broke pieces off and handed them to us. All at once, we knew who it was – it was Jesus! It was just like he did at Passover. Why hadn't we recognised him earlier? I was just about to ask him when he disappeared, as suddenly as we'd had our eyes opened!

Extraordinary happenings, but we now have no doubts that Jesus is our awaited Messiah, and alive! We agreed on the spot to return to everyone in Jerusalem. Watch this space!

Your loving friend, Mary

Continue to spend time with this story by studying a painting on the subject, such as *Supper at Emmaus* by He Qi or Caravaggio (you can find many more online).

Easter song

Poem/creative

Rise, heart, thy Lord is risen. Sing his praise
Without delays,
Who takes thee by the hand, that thou likewise
With him mayst rise:
That, as his death calcinèd thee to dust,
His life may make thee gold, and, much more, just.

Awake, my lute, and struggle for thy part
With all thy art,
The cross taught all wood to resound his name
Who bore the same.
His stretchèd sinews taught all strings what key
Is best to celebrate this most high day.

Consort, both heart and lute, and twist a song
Pleasant and long;
Or, since all music is but three parts vied
And multiplied
Oh let thy blessèd Spirit bear a part,
And make up our defects with his sweet art.

George Herbert, 1593–1633

Although the old language can be difficult to read, George Herbert's 'Easter' poem uses metaphor to great effect. He desired to use all his ability and labour to honour Jesus at Easter, whether literally on a lute, or metaphorically. The verses speak of how the cross and Christ's stretched sinews taught all wooden instruments with gut strings to glorify Jesus' name. Herbert celebrates the resurrection for turning our destined 'dust' into 'gold', and he invites the Holy Spirit to perfect his harmony (Western triad chords).

To 'twist his song', Herbert combines all his art, struggle and heart with the blessing of the Holy Spirit. What ability, effort and love might you awaken to create an offering for Jesus with the aid of the Holy Spirit? Look for a way to express your offering, be it in words, music, prayer or action.

You might want to compose your own poem using a specific method, such as the one in the example below. Sometimes fill-words, for example pronouns, are needed between:

Jesus (Line 1: a noun/object)
betrayed, tortured, crucified (Line 2: three adjectives, describing noun)
quietly, surely (Line 3: two adverbs describing the following verb)
rose (Line 4: a verb)
forever (Line 5: ending adverb)

You may wish to listen to Vaughan Williams' musical setting of George Herbert's poem on YouTube.

Choose for yourselves this day...

Sally Welch

Noah

Introduction

Read Genesis 6:5–22.

Sitting cross-legged in a circle with 20 four-year-olds, I try to make sense of the stories of the Old Testament using points of reference which will be familiar to them, drawn from their everyday experience. As I share the rich panoply of events and characters which form the bedrock of these books, one theme emerges more strongly than ever: how do we decide to live the way we do? How do we discern the principles which should undergird our actions and words? For my group of four-year-olds 'good' and 'bad' choices are a familiar concept. Children learn to take responsibility for their actions and reflect on whether they chose wisely or not, learning also to accept the consequences of these actions.

Let us too look at some of the characters from the Old Testament and examine the choices they made – and how they lived with the subsequent results. We too may gain some wisdom to help us in our daily lives to make good choices, and where better to begin than with the story of Noah, who alone chose to walk in God's path when all around were falling into dark ways, corrupt and shameful. Risking the censure and ridicule of his community, Noah listened to the voice of God calling to him in a dream and determined to act upon it.

God still speaks to us today in dreams. Try keeping a dream journal; writing each morning your memories of the night, then prayerfully asking God to reveal the truth which might lie within them.

'Speak, Lord, for your servant is listening' (1 Samuel 3:9).

Joshua

Reflective

Read Joshua 24:13–28.

The great prophet Joshua has guided Israel for many years. Now, about to die, he gives a final charge to the people he loves. Telling once again the wonderful story of the people – how God led them from slavery into the promised land – he reminds them of the good life which they now enjoy. All they must do, says Joshua, is serve the Lord – if so, they will continue to reap the benefits of the covenant. If, however, they decide to 'serve foreign gods' (v. 20), God will bring disaster on the people. The choice, says Joshua, is theirs.

During times of personal darkness, it can be very helpful to look back and remember all the occasions when God has helped us in the past. Make a faith timeline as a visual reminder of God's promises to you. Draw a horizontal and vertical axis. Label the horizontal line with your years, and the vertical line with how strongly God was apparent in the event. Draw out your faith journey, labelling significant stages or moments. This might, for example, begin with Sunday school, or a conversion experience, it might dip lower during times of doubt, or go higher when prayers were answered or when you decided to learn more about your faith, or practise prayer more diligently. There may be occasions when it seemed as if God was absent or far away. On reflection, can you discern his saving action in the event? As you look back at your journey, thank God that he has been with you always, and ask him to help you as you journey forwards.

'And the people said to Joshua: "We will serve the Lord our God and obey him"' (v. 24).

Gideon

Creative/reflective

Read Judges 6:36–40.

I was sitting in a café with my mother, many years ago, trying to decide whether it was right to take a new post which I had been offered. 'There is just the issue of James,' I said. 'I can't find a nursery for him.' My mother, ever practical, pointed out of the window at the board outside the building opposite, declaring its status as 'nursery and pre-school'. A visit and an offer of a place followed. With the final piece of the jigsaw in place I accepted the post.

Gideon too had a decision to make. After Joshua's death, things went badly for the Israelites and they were plagued by the raiding parties of the Midianites. God chose Gideon to lead the battle against them, but Gideon had a great deal of trouble in believing he was equal to the job, requiring many signs before he would put his trust in the Lord. The action of 'laying a fleece before the Lord' has been much misused down the centuries, and Jesus himself reminds us that we must 'not put the Lord your God to the test' (Luke 4:12). Nonetheless, we can be alert to the signs that God gives us to help us in our choices and decision making. These may not be as obvious as a 'dew-soaked fleece' but may arise from memories of Bible passages or guidance from books concerning the challenges we are faced with. Why not resolve to read at least one book on a subject which interests you this month? In this way your 'bank of wisdom' can gradually be increased, enabling you to make more informed choices when called upon to do so.

Naaman

Creative

Read 2 Kings 5:1–14.

Poor Naaman! A man so powerful, yet so helpless in the face of his terrible affliction. Used to the company of kings and potentates, it is mere servants who offer him the advice that will save his life – advice which he is initially too proud to accept. Luckily for Naaman, his strength of character is such that he can recognise the wisdom which is present in the words of Elisha, and because of this he is not only healed but accepts the God of Israel as the one true Lord.

When we are faced with choices and options it is very easy to be swayed by all sorts of irrelevant arguments. We confuse externally imposed judgements on what we 'ought' to do with our own feelings of what is truly right and allow worldly considerations to influence our decision making.

Take a large piece of paper and a pen or pencil and draw yourself in the middle. Place a large question mark above your head. Think of all the things which might influence you in making a decision and write them in bubbles all around your picture. Take care to include those influences which you are ashamed of, but which you know you take into account, such as personal cost, effect on social status, etc. Look at the picture you have drawn and consider what it is in you that must be set aside before God's will for you can be done. What obstructs you from fulfilling God's purposes for you?

Let me die to myself so that I may serve you;
Let me live to you who are life itself.

St Teresa of Avila, 1515–82

Ruth

Creative

Read Ruth 1:1–18.

These lines of poetry are the final answer of Ruth to Naomi, the culmination no doubt of much lengthy prayer and consideration. In them Ruth puts aside her own hopes for marriage and a fresh start in the land of her birth and instead links her destiny to that of her mother-in-law, Naomi. This decision will involve travelling to a new land, forsaking all that is familiar and risking all that she has. But Ruth has made up her mind and will not be swayed from that decision. She knows it is right for her and for Naomi.

Ultimately Ruth and Naomi both benefit but Ruth's courage and single-mindedness should not be underestimated. Sometimes the right choice is made apparent to us quite easily, at other times it is harder. Ruth would not have been at fault if she had chosen to stay and remarry in her homeland – for us too it may seem that whatever our decision it will be morally acceptable. Then we must travel, with Ruth, one stage further, and try to discern which step will enable us to serve God in the best way for us. How will our decision fit in with our calling? Which choice is not only good, but right for us?

Imagine you are called to write a short obituary for yourself. What would you like it to say about you? In no more than 150 words, what are the achievements you consider most important in your life? How would you like to be remembered? Once you have done this, you might want to refine this down to the words on your tombstone.

Looking at what you have written, which of your current activities further these things and which merely stand in their way? What action might you take to re-order your priorities?

Lot's wife

Creative

Read Genesis 19:15–26.

Making the right decisions can take an awful lot of time and effort. We can spend days researching all the possibilities which lie before us, hours talking to friends and colleagues, asking their advice and opinion on which is the best course of action to take and we can lie awake for night after night working out which option is the best for all concerned. Lot and his family had no such difficulties – given the choice of complete annihilation or escape, they fled, only just in front of the disaster that overcame their city. Once away, however, Lot's wife fell prey to that all-too-human failing, of wanting to make quite sure she had made the right decision. Looking back, she witnesses the burning sulphur raining down upon the city and for her lack of trust and faith, is turned into a pillar of salt.

A wise man once said to me when I was agonising over whether a particular decision I had made was the right one: 'Once you have planted a tree you must not keep digging it up to look at its roots or it will never grow.' Once our decisions are made, provided they have been made carefully and prayerfully, then we must trust God that our choices will bear good fruit and not look back with regret picturing what might have been.

Find pictures of runners and racers, medals and racetracks in magazines or on the internet. Make a collage of them and use this as part of your prayer today, asking God for the grace to 'run with perseverance the race marked out for us, fixing our eyes on Jesus, the pioneer and perfecter of faith' (Hebrews 12:1b, 2a).

Adam and Eve

Creative

Read Genesis 3:1–21.

It may seem strange to end this theme with an example of a bad choice, unwisely made, but of course it is often in our bad choices and decisions that we learn the most. Being made to live with the consequences of ill-thought-out actions, provoking regret or sorrow, can lead to repentance and a new direction, armed with a wisdom that is more valued because it has been so hard won. The story of Adam and Eve seems to end sadly, but it is not the end. God will not leave them, just as he will not leave us, and he will walk by their side as he does by ours, as they struggle with their new existence, making their way in a hostile world, nonetheless finding satisfaction and joy in it. Finally, in Christ, we are given the redeemer of all our past errors and misjudgements and the route forward into a new future.

Cut a slice from a piece of apple and, using the exposed face of the fruit, carefully carve out the shape of a cross. Make a print using this shape by carefully dipping the apple in a shallow bowl of paint or ink in whatever colour you like, then pressing it firmly onto paper or card. You may need to experiment a few times to get the amount of paint and the weight of pressure right. Let your finished print dry and use it during your prayer times to consider the way that God's saving action in Jesus has redeemed our fallibility and frailty. The cross of the true path has overcome the apple of many choices, giving to all who turn to Christ the hope of new life, lived in and through love.

As a Child

Phil Steer

Pray

> *This, then, is how you should pray: 'Our Father in heaven'.*
> MATTHEW 6:9, NIV

Here, of course, are the opening words of the most famous prayer in Christendom. The Lord's Prayer must have been prayed by almost every believer ever since Jesus gave it to us in response to his disciples' request, 'Lord, teach us to pray.' But, despite its familiarity (dare I say, over-familiarity), there is, I think, an important aspect of the prayer that we can easily overlook: that in praying to God as our Father we are necessarily praying to him as his children. Hence, when we come to God in prayer, we are to do so just like a child coming to his or her father, wanting to talk with him and ask something of him.

We are now so familiar with the Lord's Prayer that it is almost impossible for us to think of it being any other way. But Jesus' use of such language shocked and appalled the religious authorities of the day – and indeed, would have been hardly less shocking to any God-fearing Jew. They knew that God was to be approached as a mighty king – indeed, as the Almighty King – with fear and trembling and reverence and awe. Yet here was Jesus telling his disciples to approach God as a child approaches his father; yes, with respect, but also with confidence and joy, and the certainty of his love and care and concern.

Jesus used the same imagery in his teaching elsewhere on

prayer: 'If you then, though you are evil, know how to give good gifts to your children, how much more will your Father in heaven give good gifts to those who ask him' (Matthew 7:11). To pray like a child means to ask like a child: to come to our heavenly Father and simply ask him for what we want. This, however, is something that some of us are rather reluctant to do. We feel that it is not quite right somehow for us to come to God and just reel off a litany of requests; we believe that prayer should be so much more than this. And yes, prayer should be so much more than this. But, if we are not careful, we can make prayer so much less than this, as in our desire to pray with supposed maturity we end up neglecting the very thing that Jesus tells us to do – which is to ask for what we want.

Such an approach also has the dubious 'benefit' that the less we ask of God, the less we will be disappointed when our prayers seem to go unanswered; in this way, not praying becomes a simple and rather effective protection mechanism. But, of course, the flip-side is that the less we ask of God, the less we will rejoice and be encouraged when our prayers are answered. As James warns us, 'You do not have because you do not ask God' (James 4:2). Little children are always ready to ask their parents for help and provision; there's no hesitation or worrying about whether it is 'right' that they do so. In the intimacy and security of the parent-child relationship, to ask is the most natural thing in the world. And in the same way we, like little children, are to be always ready to turn to our heavenly Father and ask of him in prayer.

I was pondering such an approach to prayer whilst on holiday with my family. One day we went on a cycle ride and, not having a 'proper' paper map of the area, we took our sat-nav with us. Unfortunately, on setting out on our return journey we discovered that we'd somehow lost the sat-nav – and, despite much searching, it was nowhere to be found. It occurred to me that perhaps I should try putting into practice what I 'preached'; that I should do what a little child would do when he lost something, and ask my heavenly Father to help me find it. You might perhaps be unsurprised to learn that the sat-nav still didn't turn up, and we cycled back without it (fortunately the route was fairly straightforward). But this is how it is with prayer: it is not a spell or incantation that we have simply to recite in order magically to get what we want. I have absolutely no idea how or why prayer 'works' or 'doesn't work' (as we might see it) but I do know that God tells us to keep on asking nonetheless.

Indeed, such persistence is another very childlike quality that God tells us we need to have. Every parent will have experienced this with their own children: when they really want something, they just will not take 'no' for an answer!

My daughter loves animals, and she set her heart on having a pet. Now my wife and I are full of appreciation for animals in the wild; we just don't want any in the home, and so have always steadfastly resisted her pleas (except for a brief period when we 'generously' allowed her to have a couple of goldfish). Yet, despite this, our daughter was not to be deterred. She kept asking us if she could please have a hamster for her birthday, and somehow we ended up succumbing to her request. Just how did this happen?

Jesus encourages just such childlike persistence in the parable of the persistent widow (Luke 18:1-8). (Notably, there are many places in the Bible where widows and children are spoken of in the same breath, both lacking power and influence, often vulnerable and down-trodden.) Luke makes the point that Jesus told his disciples this parable in order 'to show them that they should always pray and not give up'. The widow was unable to obtain the justice that she desired because the judge had absolutely no concern for her or the righteousness of her cause. But, not to be put off, she kept on and on asking; and eventually he became so fed up with her constant badgering that he gave her what she wanted just to shut her up and get her off his back. The point of the parable is not that God is like that unjust judge, but rather that if he 'who neither feared God nor cared about men' eventually responded to the widow's persistence, how much more should we persist in praying to our loving heavenly Father, who delights to give good things to his children?

And this is why our daughter received a hamster for her birthday: not because she wore us down with her asking, but rather because her persistence showed us just how much she desired a pet, and we realised that we wanted to give her the joy and happiness it would bring.

So does this mean that God needs to see our persistence in prayer in order to prove the strength of our desire for what we ask? To be honest, I don't know. I suspect that this may at times be one part of the mystery that is prayer, but it is by no means as simple and straightforward as that. All I do know is that God tells us to ask like little children, and to keep asking like little children, and to trust him, as our loving heavenly Father, to answer.

Such persistence does not mean, however, that we have to use long, wordy prayers that go on and on. Indeed, Jesus specifically tells us not to 'keep on babbling', thinking that we will be heard because of our many words, 'for your Father knows what you need before you ask him' (Matthew 6:8). It is not long prayers but frequent prayers that our Father seeks; not to pray and forget, but to pray and to pray; to keep the object of our prayers close to our heart and to the forefront of our mind, that we might keep turning to him and asking him to grant us those things that we seek.

Incidentally, when we returned from our cycle ride, the missing sat-nav turned up in one of the bags that we'd taken with us and had searched so thoroughly earlier. Coincidence? Quite possibly. All I can say for certain is that I had asked God to help me find it, and now here it was. You might balk at the idea of a God who apparently locates lost sat-navs when so many much more important prayers – about sickness and disease, poverty and famine, conflict and war – seemingly go unanswered. And in many ways I would share such sentiments; indeed, I hesitated over whether I should mention the episode at all. Yet this is the typical concern of an adult; little children are not bothered about whether what they ask for is 'important' or 'significant' enough. They simply ask out of the reality of their felt needs and desires, and are thankful when their requests are answered.

This is not to say, of course, that we should be childish in our prayers, asking for anything and everything that we want; as James warns us, if we seek simply to satisfy our own selfish desires, then we should not expect to receive the things for which we ask. Nonetheless, it must surely be better to pray for many things, even if some of them are 'wrong', than to pray for too little. And so we are to ask with a childlike confidence, praying 'on all occasions with all kinds of prayers and requests', being thankful and encouraged by all answered prayer, no matter how seemingly trivial. And we are to keep on asking for those more important things that we have yet to receive, having a childlike persistence born out of a heart-felt desire for God's kingdom to come more and more in our lives, in the church and in the world.

Thought about going on retreat?

Alison MacTier

Technology has given us a great many benefits that our grandparents could only have dreamed of – allowing us to fit more and more into our days. The only problem with this is that the majority of us prefer not to stop for fear of losing our place or of missing out. It has left us with a kind of secret yearning for permission to get off the treadmill, take a few deep breaths and find an alternative way of being. But by listening to this natural inclination within us, we could be embarking on a life-changing journey.

There is a common misunderstanding that retreats are only for the most prayerful and holy among us. We may have picked up a few notions of religious communities – their discipline, structure, serenity – for which we have a high regard, but in which we may feel we can have no part. What we may be missing is an invitation into something which is much more universal than we imagined.

While the history of going on retreat is rooted in religious community, it has more recently diversified in ways that are more accessible to the contemporary world. Christian retreat centres today vary enormously in size, facilities, location and programme. But they have in common a tradition of daily prayer and a hospitality which is welcoming to all – at whatever stage of the spiritual journey the visitor may be. They offer a comfortable space, predominantly en-suite guest rooms, high-quality meals, homely sitting areas, libraries in which to read or reflect, and often beautiful gardens to wander in.

A fear of silence can inhibit us from crossing the retreat threshold but not all retreats are silent, nor are they solitary. You could choose, for example, to go on a retreat with a specific emphasis on the Christian seasons of Lent or Advent, on a spiritual writer or biblical text, or you could try a retreat focusing on a specific hobby such as poetry or music. Retreats like these offer companionship and the opportunity to meet and share with others.

Retreats can also offer a safe space in which to find support and advice when facing a particular challenge in life. A number of retreat centres offer retreats for those finding themselves in a crisis such as relationship breakdown, a time of change, or caring for a loved one who is sick.

While a retreat shared with others may be helpful and appropriate in many circumstances, there is also no replacing the experience of silence and solitude, where there is time and space to encounter God and also something of yourself that is unique, precious and life-affirming. For such retreats you may like to do your own thing or you may want to try an 'individually guided retreat' in which you meet regularly with a trained guide who can offer you suggestions for reading and reflection.

If all this seems too daunting a prospect or more than your diary can realistically accommodate, you might consider attending a Quiet Day as an alternative. Many retreat centres offer a number of these days in their annual programme. They are like a shorter version of a retreat – offering some input while allowing you space and silence for your own reflection. Quiet Days are a great way of introducing more time for reflection into your life without having to plan for several days away.

Taking time out away from the familiarity of home and daily routine allows us space to look at things in a new way. But there are also other ways in which you can continue this journey in daily life. One of these is by sharing your experiences with a spiritual director or companion. The emphasis here is very much on you but your director may be able to shed some light on what they have heard and offer insights. They will be trained to listen to whatever is going on for you at that time and offer suggestions for the way ahead.

Going on retreat or finding a spiritual director for the first time can be a daunting prospect and the Retreat Association is here to help you navigate the process. We can give you advice and offer you some suggestions for where to go and who to contact. Above all, we hope to encourage you in finding your own pathway towards a place of reflection. Deciding to take a step back from our busy 24/7 world could be one of the best decisions you've ever made!

Alison MacTier is the Executive Director of the Retreat Association, a national Christian charity which aims to help people find a retreat or space for reflection in their lives. Its work includes providing resources, events, training and regular, impartial advice to all enquirers. The Retreat Association publishes the *Retreats* handbook every December, listing over 230 retreat centres across and beyond the UK. For more details, please see **www.retreats.org.uk** or phone 01494 569056.

BRF Quiet Days

Jesus said, 'Come with me by yourselves to a quiet place.'
Mark 6:31 (NIV)

BRF Quiet Days are an ideal way of redressing the balance in our busy lives. Held in peaceful locations around the country, each one is led by an experienced speaker and gives the opportunity to reflect, be silent and pray, and, through it all, to draw closer to God.

BRF also offers other events throughout the year:

Women's conferences
In conjunction with *Woman Alive* magazine, these conferences offer inspiring speakers and worship with thought-provoking workshops which focus on the spirituality of women.

Festival of Prayer
A day to explore different aspects of spirituality and prayer, organised with the Diocese of Oxford.

For further details and to book, please go to
brfonline.org.uk/events-and-quiet-days

Quiet Spaces
Prayer Journal

80 Creative
Prayer
Ideas
A resource for church
and group use
Claire Daniel

To order

Online: **brfonline.org.uk**
Tel.: +44 (0)1865 319700
Mon–Fri 9.15–17.30

Delivery times within the UK are normally 15 working days. Prices are correct at the time of going to press but may change without prior notice.

BRF

Title	Price	Qty	Total
Quiet Spaces Prayer Journal	£9.99		
40 Days with the Celtic Saints	£7.99		
80 Creative Prayer Ideas	£8.99		

POSTAGE AND PACKING CHARGES			
Order value	**UK**	**Europe**	**Rest of world**
Under £7.00	£2.00	£5.00	£7.00
£7.00–£29.99	£3.00	£9.00	£15.00
£30.00 and over	FREE	£9.00 + 15% of order value	£15.00 + 20% of order value

Total value of books	
Postage and packing	
Total for this order	

Please complete in BLOCK CAPITALS

Title .... First name/initials .... Surname ....

Address ....

.... Postcode ....

Acc. No. .... Telephone ....

Email ....

Please keep me informed about BRF's books and resources ❑ by email ❑ by post
Please keep me informed about the wider work of BRF ❑ by email ❑ by post

Method of payment

❑ Cheque (made payable to BRF) ❑ MasterCard / Visa

Card no. ☐☐☐☐ ☐☐☐☐ ☐☐☐☐ ☐☐☐☐

Valid from M M Y Y Expires M M Y Y Security code* ☐☐☐
Last 3 digits on the reverse of the card

Signature* .... Date ..../......./.......

*ESSENTIAL IN ORDER TO PROCESS YOUR ORDER

Please return this form with the appropriate payment to:

BRF, 15 The Chambers, Vineyard, Abingdon OX14 3FE | enquiries@brf.org.uk

To read our terms and find out about cancelling your order, please visit **brfonline.org.uk/terms**.

QS0118

QUIET SPACES SUBSCRIPTION FORM

All our Bible reading notes can be ordered online by visiting **biblereadingnotes.org.uk/subscriptions**

If you and a minimum of **four** friends subscribe to *Quiet Spaces* or BRF's other Bible reading notes (*New Daylight*, *Day by Day with God*, *Guidelines*, *The Upper Room*), you can form a group. What's so good about being in a group? You pay the price of the notes only – postage is free for delivery to a UK address. (All notes are sent to one address.) All group orders are invoiced. No advance payment is required. For more information, visit **biblereadingnotes.org.uk/group-subscriptions** or contact the BRF office.

Title ---------- First name/initials ------------- Surname ------------------------------------

Address --

-- Postcode ----------------------

Telephone -------------------------- Email --

INDIVIDUAL SUBSCRIPTION Please send *Quiet Spaces* beginning with the May 2018 / September 2018 / January 2019 issue (*delete as appropriate*):

	Quantity	UK	Europe	Rest of world
(per 3 issues)	☐	☐ £16.95	☐ £25.20	☐ £29.10

Total enclosed £ ----------------- (cheques should be made payable to 'BRF')

Please charge my MasterCard / Visa ☐ Debit card ☐ with £ ----------------

Card no. ☐☐☐☐ ☐☐☐☐ ☐☐☐☐ ☐☐☐☐

Valid from M M Y Y Expires M M Y Y Security code* ☐☐☐

Last 3 digits on the reverse of the card

Signature* -- Date ------/------/------

*ESSENTIAL IN ORDER TO PROCESS YOUR ORDER

To set up a Direct Debit, please also complete the Direct Debit instruction on the reverse of this form.

GROUP SUBSCRIPTION (UK only) Please send *Quiet Spaces* beginning with the May 2018 / September 2018 / January 2019 issue (*delete as appropriate*):

Quantity ☐ (Current price per issue: £4.50)

Please invoice me: per issue / annually (*delete as appropriate*).

Please return this form to:

BRF, 15 The Chambers, Vineyard, Abingdon OX14 3FE

To read our terms and find out about cancelling your order, please visit **brfonline.org.uk/terms**.

The Bible Reading Fellowship is a Registered Charity (233280)

QS0118

The Bible Reading Fellowship

Instruction to your bank or building society to pay by Direct Debit

Please fill in the whole form using a ballpoint pen and return it to:
BRF, 15 The Chambers, Vineyard, Abingdon OX14 3FE

Service User Number: | 5 | 5 | 8 | 2 | 2 | 9 |

Name and full postal address of your bank or building society

To: The Manager	Bank/Building Society
Address	
	Postcode

Name(s) of account holder(s)

Branch sort code

Bank/Building Society account number

Reference number

Instruction to your Bank/Building Society

Please pay The Bible Reading Fellowship Direct Debits from the account detailed in this instruction, subject to the safeguards assured by the Direct Debit Guarantee. I understand that this instruction may remain with The Bible Reading Fellowship and, if so, details will be passed electronically to my bank/building society.

Signature(s)

Banks and Building Societies may not accept Direct Debit instructions for some types of account.

DIRECT DEBIT PAYMENT

You can pay for your annual subscription to our Bible reading notes using Direct Debit. You need only give your bank details once, and the payment is made automatically every year until you cancel it. If you would like to pay by Direct Debit, please use the form opposite, entering your BRF account number under 'Reference number'.

You are fully covered by the Direct Debit Guarantee:

The Direct Debit Guarantee

- This Guarantee is offered by all banks and building societies that accept instructions to pay Direct Debits.
- If there are any changes to the amount, date or frequency of your Direct Debit, The Bible Reading Fellowship will notify you 10 working days in advance of your account being debited or as otherwise agreed. If you request The Bible Reading Fellowship to collect a payment, confirmation of the amount and date will be given to you at the time of the request.
- If an error is made in the payment of your Direct Debit, by The Bible Reading Fellowship or your bank or building society, you are entitled to a full and immediate refund of the amount paid from your bank or building society.
- If you receive a refund you are not entitled to, you must pay it back when The Bible Reading Fellowship asks you to.
- You can cancel a Direct Debit at any time by simply contacting your bank or building society. Written confirmation may be required. Please also notify us.

How to encourage Bible reading in your church

BRF has been helping individuals connect with the Bible for over 90 years. We want to support churches as they seek to encourage church members into regular Bible reading.

Order a Bible reading resources pack

This pack is designed to give your church the tools to publicise our Bible reading notes. It includes:

- Sample Bible reading notes for your congregation to try.
- Publicity resources, including a poster.
- A church magazine feature about Bible reading notes.

The pack is free, but we welcome a £5 donation to cover the cost of postage. If you require a pack to be sent outside the UK or require a specific number of sample Bible reading notes, please contact us for postage costs. More information about what the current pack contains is available on our website.

How to order and find out more

- Visit **biblereadingnotes.org.uk/for-churches**.
- Telephone BRF on +44 (0)1865 319700 Mon–Fri 9.15–17.30.
- Write to us at BRF, 15 The Chambers, Vineyard, Abingdon OX14 3FE.

Keep informed about our latest initiatives

We are continuing to develop resources to help churches encourage people into regular Bible reading, wherever they are on their journey. Join our email list at **biblereadingnotes.org.uk/helpingchurches** to stay informed about the latest initiatives that your church could benefit from.

Introduce a friend to our notes

We can send information about our notes and current prices for you to pass on. Please contact us.